Jewels of Somerset

Stained Glass in Parish Churches from 1830

HUGH PLAYFAIR

design & photography - Chris Akroyd

Preface

by **Jill Kerr Channer** MA FSA FRSA IHBC
Architectural Glass Historian,
Secretary of the *Corpus Vitrearum Medii
Aevi Great Britain* 1975-1984

MINEHEAD ST MICHAEL
The Boy Jesus by Henry Holiday

This book is a revelation.

It continues the pioneering work begun over half a century ago by Christopher Woodforde's *Stained Glass in Somerset 1250-1830* – his *'contribution to the history of one of the most pleasant of English counties and one of the most interesting of the arts'* (PREFACE). This too is written as both a record and commentary *'for the local historian and topographer'*; it extends the timeline from 1830 to the present and is presented in an accessible, authoritative, informative style which speaks at many levels to a wider world.

Starting with an elegant and expertly compressed summary of all you need to know about the history, technology, development, aesthetic, techniques, identification of styles and skills required for the production and appreciation of stained and painted pictorial architectural glass, you are now equipped to embark upon your own exploration in the company of an erudite, eloquent and, occasionally, wickedly provocative guide.

The illuminating illustrations and index alone testify to the remarkable range of subjects selected – and the national, international, regional and local artists and designers commissioned by Somerset people of all ranks, ages, resources and tastes. Together they have produced the only works of art required to keep the weather out of places of worship of all periods. Such commissions were – and are to this day – a rare opportunity for an ordinary citizen to commission a commemoration to be appreciated and conserved in a public place of record. It is a matter of regret that so few church guides record the detail of these generous gifts – especially the name of the artist/designer. It is even more frustrating that so few artists sign and date their windows, which means that publications such as this are scarce because they require rigorous research, insight, knowledge – and a discerning eye.

All these attributes are skilfully and seductively deployed in these pages. All the major national nineteenth century partnership production studios are introduced by succinct summaries referencing Somerset examples of top London companies – **Burlison and Grylls**, **Clayton & Bell**, **Heaton, Butler and Bayne**, **Lavers, Barraud and Westlake**, **Morris and Company**, **James Powell and Sons** and many more, all well represented, described and illustrated. You will encounter the two international best sellers of stained glass designs by catalogues – **Mayer** of Munich and **Capronnier** of Brussels – as well as two very local artists, the **Horwood Brothers** of Mells and Frome, and **John Toms** of Wellington. The regional studios and workshops at Exeter, Bristol and Birmingham will become familiar to you, and you will enjoy recognising individual artists and designers from the grandfather of the Gothic revival, **Thomas Willement**, the revivalist leaders **William Wailes**, **Augustus Pugin** and **John Hardman** to the prolific exponents of the style such as **Henry Holiday** and **Charles Kempe**.

Above all you will be astonished by the skill and diversity of designs, styles, subject matter and techniques of the twentieth century and contemporary artists you will be introduced to. Here are the great national stars – **Ninian Comper**, **Christopher Webb**, **Hugh Easton**, **Margaret Rope**, **Martin Travers**, **Eddie Nuttgens**, **John Hayward**, **Henry Haig**, **Brian Thomas**, **Karl Parsons**, **Leonard Walker** – alongside influential, contemporary present and former south-westerners, **Tom Denny**, **Mark Angus**, the **Kettlewells**, the **Gilroys** – and still Somerset based, **Sally Pollitzer** and **Patrick Reyntiens**.

A typical example of the pleasures in store is the gazetteer entry for East Coker. There are stained glass windows commemorating the local Bullock family of sailmakers – by **Hardmans** of 1885 and **Powell and Sons** of the 1920s. As you would expect from the association with the burial place of the poet T S Eliot's ashes, there is an Eliot association in the glass, but it turns out to be the somewhat unexpected commemoration of the Eliot family's emigration to Massachusetts around 1660 commissioned in 1936 from the daringly unusual slab glass specialist, **Leonard Walker** (1879-1965). One longs to know the back story. Was Eliot himself involved? Who commissioned and paid for it? How was Walker chosen? A further surprising inducement for an irresistible visit is a two-light window in the south transept remembering six local parishioners by **Jasper and Molly Kettlewell** who had a stained glass studio at Coker Court in 1984.

But this generous publication offers more than a gazetteer for the general or specialist reader. It is a rich resource for present and future artists and commissioners of contemporary commemorations in glass. It should be required reading for all aspiring and practising stained glass artists and the very few surviving schools of art which still retain architectural glass departments. All architects and surveyors on Diocesan approved lists would benefit from acquiring a copy to demonstrate the art of the possible – and every Diocesan Advisory Committee should retain a reference copy as an exemplar and inspiration. Chapter Five with its wise words on context and functionality should be compulsory reading for all individuals involved with advising or taking decisions on introducing new stained glass designs in places of worship. As Chairman of the Diocesan Advisory Committee for Bath and Wells, with a wide and deep holistic understanding of the decision making process, the author has given us and the churches of Somerset a stunning legacy of stained glass.

'Only those who live most vividly
in the present deserve to inherit the past.'

John Russell on John & Myfanwy Piper
*From Sickert to 1948: the Achievement of the Contemporary
Arts Society 1948*

List of Photographs

Published by Beaufort Press
ISBN 978 - 0 - 9520483 - 4 - 3

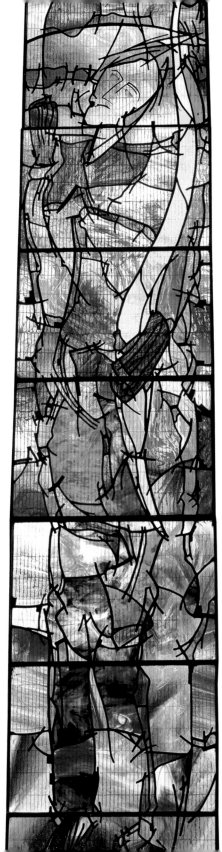

BATH LANSDOWN ST STEPHEN
St Stephen by Mark Angus

Contents

Sponsors

Anonymous
Michael Armstrong
Jennifer Beazley
Beech Tyldesley
Ken Biggs Charitable Trust
Chedburn Dudley
Penny Cudmore
Ian Hay Davison CBE
David Dixon
Andrew Drysdale
Ellis and Company
Pauline English
The Glaziers Trust
Jessamy Griffiths
Holy Well Glass
Tony Male CMG
Matthews Wrightson Charity Trust
Porter Dodson Solicitors
The Right Reverend Peter Price
Anthony Pugh-Thomas
The Venerable John Reed
George Renwick
Jonathan Rhind Architects
Chris Romain Architecture
Alan & Ann Thomas Architects
Simon Tudway-Quilter
John Wood
Angela Yeoman OBE DL

TAUNTON ST MARY MAGDALENE
The Last Judgement by Alexander Gibbs

Introduction

Christopher Woodforde's definitive book on *Somerset Stained Glass from* 1250 *to* 1830 was published in 1946, but there is no book which covers the period since 1830. *Jewels of Somerset* does not pretend to be a definitive account of stained glass since 1830 – there are simply too many churches and too many windows to cover. It is rather a celebration of and an introduction to stained glass in Somerset parish churches from 1830 to the present day. Inevitably choices have been made and there are many churches whose stained glass windows might have been included. For such omissions and for any unintended errors I take full responsibility.

There are six chapters. The first describes the role of stained glass windows. The second outlines developments since 1830. In the third there are short notes on some of the main studios. The fourth visits sixty churches with interesting stained glass. Recent commissions are listed in chapter five. Finally a score of interesting and favourite windows are included in chapter six. As far as possible I have attached to each window notes to include the number of main lights, the date either approximate (which is often the date of the death of the person commemorated) or exact, a brief description of the subject, and the artist or studio responsible. Often it is not possible to attribute a window to a particular studio and where that is the case no artist's or studio's name appears.

FOOTNOTE *The Very Reverend Christopher Woodforde, 1907-62, was Dean of Wells and a distant kinsman of Parson James Woodforde, author of* The Diary of a Country Parson, *who was born in Ansford where his father was rector.*

There is no mention of the name of the donor or person commemorated for that information appears on either the window itself or a tablet nearby.

I am deeply grateful for help, advice and encouragement from many people especially from Jill Channer, Jim Cheshire, Peter Cormack, Julian Orbach, Anthony Pugh-Thomas, Patrick Reyntiens, Jill Wrightson, and friends and colleagues on the Committee of the Friends of Somerset Churches and Chapels, and the Bath and Wells Diocesan Advisory Committee for the Care of Churches of which I was Chairman 1994-2011. I am particularly indebted to my friend and colleague Chris Akroyd, who has taken the photographs and designed the book. Any merit which the book may have is almost entirely due to his enthusiasm and professionalism. I am also very grateful for the wonderful generosity of sponsors without which the book would not have seen the light of day. They are listed opposite. All proceeds from sales will go to the Friends of Somerset Churches and Chapels.

Hugh Playfair

he is not here   for he is risen   as he said

TO MAJOR GENERAL JOHN HOWARD   MICHELL CB ROYAL ARTILLARY   WHO DIED MARCH 7 1883
ERECTED BY HIS WIFE   CAROLINE ANNE MICHELL   IN LOVING MEMORY

CHAPTER ONE

The Stained Glass Window

'To enter...a Christian church is to enter none other than the House of God and the Gate of Heaven'. So wrote **Sir Ninian Comper** in *Of the Atmosphere of a Church* published in 1947. Essentially a church is a House of God and for that reason it is filled with the finest offerings that benefactors, artists and craftsmen can give back to God in celebration and gratitude for the gifts they have so bountifully received. Such offerings include stained glass windows. **Carola Hicks** wrote, *'The beauty of glass turned the interiors of church or chapel into the Holy City of Jerusalem, as imagined in St John's vision in the Book of Revelation'.*

ALL windows, but particularly stained glass windows, are important integral features of any church building. They are not mere adornments. **Christopher Whall**, the stained glass artist, wrote, *'There must be nothing out of harmony with the architecture'*. The church architect **Stephen Dykes Bower** wrote, *'Stained glass is intrinsically linked with architecture. It may, and should, be a superlative adornment quietly radiating beauty. Union of the two must be such that each helps the other to give delight and thus earn more affection'*. Stained glass windows should be neither mere pictures nor abstract puzzles and their beauty should enhance the church for prayer and worship. Windows of indifferent quality can seriously damage the whole atmosphere of a church.

Windows serve the practical purpose of keeping out weather and letting in light. Their tracery and glazing form part of the architecture of the building. Although the original purpose of stained glass windows was to enhance the church to the Glory of God, they were in the Middle Ages important as teaching aids acting as the poor man's Bible. Their story and their symbolism helped to teach the Faith and preach the Gospel. Today, in contrast, stained glass artists often design abstract windows to create atmosphere or to explore spiritual truths in new ways. But stained glass windows also produce dazzling visual effects according to the time of day and the quality of the sunlight. In this way they transform ordinary light into heavenly light. They have magical and divine qualities which resonate with those who view them and study them. So they may be considered as jewels embellishing the Heavenly City of

HUISH EPISCOPI ST MARY
The Women at the Empty Tomb by Mayer & Company

Jerusalem. In the 12th century **Suger**, Abbot of St Denis near Paris and Counsellor to the Kings of France, claimed that stained glass was God's preferred art form.

Today most stained glass windows are memorial windows given by generous donors and dedicated in the first instance to the Glory of God. In the 19th century they came to replace stone and plaster monuments as the most useful and usual gift with which a patron could embellish a church to the Glory

of God and in memory of special people or special occasions. Abbot Suger declared that the more you spent on stained glass the better your chances of getting to Heaven!

The position of stained glass windows in a church is by no means random and only in exceptional circumstances should they be moved from the place for which they were originally theologically and architecturally designed. Traditionally windows have been grouped together with New Testament

stories and related Old Testament stories typologically side by side as in Wells St Thomas by **Wailes**, or opposite each other, the Old Testament on the north side and the New Testament on the south side of the church, as in Wraxall All Saints by **Kempe** and Blagdon St Andrew by **Powell and Sons**. The main east window usually features Our Lord in Glory either on the Cross, or as part of the Holy Trinity, or in a Nativity scene. In Somerset there are some magnificent east windows, for example in Bath Abbey, Taunton St James, and North Cadbury St Michael, all by **Clayton and Bell**. Some churches have collections of windows by particular artists or studios, for example Frome Holy Trinity by **Morris and Company**, Downside Abbey, East Clevedon All Saints, and Witham Friary all by **Comper**, Compton Pauncefoot St Mary and Corton Denham St Andrew by **Capronnier**, East Chinnock St Mary by **Gunter Anton**, and Stoke St Mary by **Patrick Reyntiens**.

Glass was first made by the Egyptians some 6,000 years ago, but translucent glass may have first appeared in Roman times a mere 2,000 years ago. Interestingly Roman glass was more robust than Medieval glass. Those who make glass and those who paint glass and design windows for churches are highly skilled craftsmen and artists, more highly regarded in the past than in the 19th century and today. In the words of Patrick Reyntiens, 'One must not only be an artist involving individuality, freedom and spontaneity, a superb colourist, a brilliant draughtsman, but also a disciplined, skilled craftsman with detailed technical proficiency and physical strength'.

Traditionally glass is made of a mixture of two parts of sand and one part of ash with a dash of lime. The mixture is heated up in a fireproof clay pot into a sticky mass. It is then blown or moulded into slabs or sheets of glass and allowed to cool in a process called *annealing*. *Muff glass* is made by blowing the molten mixture into a cylindrical shape before splitting it along its length, flattening it out, and cutting it into panels. On the other hand *crown glass* is made by blowing the molten mixture into a balloon shape, then cutting off the end and spinning it

into a disc, which is then cut into panels. *Pressed glass* is made by pouring molten glass into moulds. *Slab glass* is made by blowing molten glass into a square mould thus creating five slabs of glass. Modern *sheet glass* is made by putting molten glass through rollers. All these methods produce white glass which has a greenish tinge caused by impurities.

Coloured glass is produced by a number of different methods. The skill of the stained glass artist lies in harnessing these

3

STOKE ST MARY

FAR LEFT *The Annunciation* LEFT *St Anne teaching the Virgin Mary to read*
RIGHT *The Day of Pentecost*. Details from the series of windows by Patrick Reyntiens

NYNEHEAD ALL SAINTS
'Hope' by Sir Joshua Reynolds

techniques. **John Piper** described this art as *'painting with coloured light'*. *Pot metal glass*, so called because colourants are added to the pot of molten glass, is produced by adding metallic oxides to the formula. A favourite is *ruby glass* – red glass made by adding copper, or gold in the case of the most expensive glass. Blue glass is achieved by adding cobalt, purple by adding manganese, and greens and yellow by adding iron. F*lashing*, by dipping a ball of one colour into another, originally pot metal into molten white glass, produces glass in two layers and two colours, a thin layer of one colour *flashed* across the surface of a thicker layer, thus providing both clarity and colour. *Ruby glass* is always flashed. By *abrading*, a sort of scraping, flashed glass it is possible to make variations of shade and texture, or by removing some flashing altogether it is possible to achieve two colours without lead lines. This can also be achieved by acid etching.

A second means of colouring glass is by *silver staining*, a process discovered and developed in the 14th century. Silver nitrate is applied to white glass and fired. This produces, depending on the base glass, the strength of stain, and the length and temperature of the firing, an attractive lemon to amber or orange colour more delicate than pot metal yellow.

The third way of producing colour in a stained glass window is by *enamelling* or painting, but stained glass coloured in this way does not last as well as pot metal glass. Enamelling was particularly popular in the 18th century when painterly windows, clear glass painted with coloured enamels, aped the art of the portrait and landscape painters. All enamels are basically ground glass with a medium such as lavender oil or gum arabic. Brown enamel enables the glass painter to draw lines and apply shading before glass is fired. Usually stained glass is pot metal painted or shaded with enamels as in Medieval and Victorian times.

The skill of the stained glass artist involves the designing, colouring, painting, staining and installing of glass produced by the glass maker. First a sketch is produced before a cartoon and template of the image or pattern is drawn out, which must be approved by the donor, the Church and other interested parties. The various pieces of glass are then cut into shape with a *grozing iron*, or *diamond* (since the 17th century, after which both were used, the former for curves and the latter for straight lines), or *steel wheel* (since the 19th century). Finally the pieces are painted and fired before being put together and cemented in H-shaped lead *calmes*. These calmes and *ferrous saddle bars* to secure larger windows all involve the artist's care and ingenuity for they are part of the design process. Not all church windows are made of stained glass. Many delightful windows have clear glass and intricate glazing patterns using *quarries*, small pieces of glass, usually of diamond shape. Such windows with appropriate *ferramenta* and glass of suitable thickness and texture not only let in light but are also less expensive and allow a view of the immediate landscape. *Grisaille* (from the French word *gris* meaning grey) windows, without an image, often have patterns (geometric, floral, or *diaper*) in clear or muted coloured glass. They can be rich in pattern and colour with appropriately patterned leading as for example in **Charlton Mackrell St Mary** and **Wells St Thomas**. Sometimes such windows have in their centre roundels, or medallions, or scrolls.

CHAPTER TWO

Revival & Development

THE Medieval art and craft of stained glass, which reached its zenith in England in the early 16th century, was destroyed by the Protestant Reformation in the reigns of Henry VIII and Edward VI. It was not revived until the Gothic Revival led by **A W N Pugin** some 300 years later. Many Medieval churches were filled with stained glass. Some may have been quite dark inside, but in the 15th century churches became lighter as Perpendicular windows became larger, almost walls of glass as in the east end of Bath Abbey. But Protestants, especially the zealots, regarded stained glass windows as idolatrous. Consequently not only were stained glass windows no longer made but existing windows were smashed, especially by the iconoclasts of Edward VI's reign. Those that survived were almost all destroyed by order of Parliament in Cromwellian times a century later. Negligence and ignorance have also taken their toll over the years. Normally only fragments of the glorious stained glass of Medieval churches survive. Such remnants can be seen in the traceries of many Somerset churches.

The art of making stained glass was lost until it was rediscovered in the 19th century. Some 'stained' glass windows were made – armorial windows and in the 18th century painterly windows designed and painted as pictures, but they were neither as vibrant nor as enduring as the stained glass windows of the Middle Ages. Painterly glass can be seen in the **Reynolds** windows in the chancel of Nynehead All Saints.

The rediscovery of the constituents and the means of making glass as in the Middle Ages came with the growing interest in Gothic architecture which was seen as the most appropriate style for building churches to accommodate the growing population of Industrial Revolution England. Of course existing Medieval churches and surviving Medieval glass also needed repair. A good example of a restored Medieval stained glass window in Somerset is the east window of Langport All Saints. The great exponent of the Gothic Revival of the 1840s and 1850s was Pugin, who built his first church in 1837. With the Romantic Movement there came a huge revival of interest in medieval art and architecture. In the 1830s the **Oxford Movement** and the **Cambridge Camden Society** led to a revival of interest in Anglo-Catholic liturgy and the creation of church buildings suitable for such liturgy. The Cambridge Camden Society's journal *The Ecclesiologist*, first published in 1841, was particularly significant in influencing the building and furnishing of churches in a programme of church building and restoration which was a hallmark of Victorian England. As a consequence the art of stained glass in England reached a new height not seen since the Middle Ages. Only three glass painters were listed in the census of 1831, but by 1851 there were 531. There were probably many more. The demand for stained glass reached a peak in the 1870s and did not decline until World War I. In his book on Norfolk stained glass Birkin Haward states that nationally some 80,000 windows were made for 15,000 churches in the 19th century.

The break-through in the making of *antique* 'Medieval' glass came in the 1840s when **Pugin**, **Charles Winston**, **Joseph Bell** of Bristol and others were looking for glass suitable for the

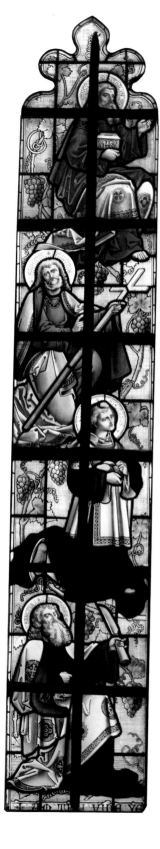

restoration of Medieval windows. The *antiquating* of existing glass was not satisfactory to Pugin so he persuaded **Hardman and Company** to contact **James Hartley** of Sunderland who was making an antique crown glass which emulated Medieval glass. Charles Winston, an amateur stained glass enthusiast, also knew of Hartley's glass and persuaded **James Powell and Sons** of Whitefriars to make antique glass to a recipe concocted by himself and the chemist **Medlock**. This glass was first used by **Ward and Hughes** in 1852. James Powell and Sons made Winston's glass as well as their own muff glass but eventually the two were combined into their own antique muff glass. At the same time **W E Chance** of Birmingham was making antique muff glass for Hardman and Company. There followed a great period of English glass making with three of the main Victorian stained glass firms **Clayton and Bell**; **Heaton, Butler** (later **and Bayne**); and **Lavers, Barraud** (later **and Westlake**) all using glass influenced by Powell's experiments. Other manufacturers were also making antique glass. It is quite possible that some of the glass used by Clayton and Bell was made by James Hartley rather than by Powell as assumed! There are many good examples of the work of these and other Victorian firms in Somerset churches.

The quality of the stained glass varied both in design and in performance. Much early Victorian glass is predictable, unimaginative and imitative of the glass of the Middle Ages, at first in single lights figures beneath a canopy, as at **Butleigh St Leonard** in **Thomas Willement's** east window of as early as 1829. As a result of short cuts in the firing process, especially with the introduction of borax, many windows have suffered serious paint loss. Some firms were more affected than others. Stained glass artists were very much constrained not only by the quality of glass but also by subservience to the great Victorian architects, who wanted windows designed to match the particular Gothic style they were adopting. The practice of including canopies in the design helped windows blend with the architecture, an important consideration as studios would not necessarily have been familiar with the building for which they were making the glass.

7

NYNEHEAD ALL SAINTS
A Selection of Saints by Frederick Drake

sanctus lucas

8

Developments in the making of glass were accompanied by changes in taste and in the design of stained glass windows. Reverence for Gothic architecture and Medieval stained glass declined in the 1860s with the foundation of the firm eventually known as **Morris and Company** in 1861. At first a devotee Morris later moved away from the Gothic style. Especially influential was **Edward Burne-Jones**, friend of **Ruskin**, the defender of the **Pre-Raphaelites** – Rossetti, Holman Hunt and Millais. With their interest in God, the Middle Ages, the natural world and new ideas, the influence of the pre-Raphaelites on religious art from 1848 was enormous. Designs became more secular with Pre-Raphaelite figures and backgrounds of foliage. Lead lines became more important and colours softer with much use of silver stain. Clear glass was used to let in as much light as possible. The stained glass artist was more in control of his craft. Most studios followed the trend, but some remained traditional in approach.

A new golden age of English stained glass began in the 1890s with the introduction of *slab* glass. This glass of variable thickness and colour, made by Powell and Sons and by Hartley Wood, was expensive but more interesting and versatile, a fact readily exploited by the **Arts and Crafts Movement** of the 1880s led in stained glass by **Christopher Whall**, who was much influenced by Morris and Burne-Jones. The Arts and Crafts Movement in turn had a huge impact on the stained glass artists **Henry Holiday**, **Nathaniel Westlake**, **Ninian Comper**, **Martin Travers** and others. Many of their windows can be seen in Somerset churches.

FROME HOLY TRINITY
St Luke by Edward Burne-Jones

In the 20th century there has been some decline in the quantity and the quality of church stained glass windows, though there are notable exceptions. World War I was critical in this decline as the world became more secular, church going declined, windows filled, and many of the main glass making firms ceased to exist. Chance stopped making glass in the 1940s, Powell in the 1970s, and Hartley Wood in the 1990s. Two contrasting styles have developed as artists have thrown off the shackles of being true to architecture and the traditional subjects of the Bible, the Christian Faith, and the lives of saints. The more traditional and conventional artists, such as **Henry Holiday**, **Ninian Comper**, **Martin Travers**, **F C Eden**, **Hugh Easton**, **John Hayward**, **Patrick Reyntiens** and **Jane Gray**, have retained a representational approach. Others, such as **Mark Angus** and **Tom Denny**, have followed a more abstract approach exploring Faith and creating atmosphere. It has been well said that windows should let in light and either elucidate or decorate. Some new windows sit uncomfortably in the historic churches they inhabit for the sound advice of **Christopher Whall** is not always followed. '*Do not try crude experiments on venerable and beautiful buildings, but be modest and reticent; know the styles of the past thoroughly and add your own fresh feeling to them reverently. And in thought do not think it necessary to be novel in order to be original*'. The commissioning of new windows continues apace for although church-going may have declined interest in churches is very much alive.

WINSCOMBE ST JAMES
Tree of Jesse by William Burges

CHAPTER THREE

Artists & Studios of the Revival

The fifteen studios described here, mainly in London, produced probably over half of the stained glass windows installed in Somerset between 1830 and 1914.

MILVERTON ST MICHAEL
Jesus carrying the Cross with Saints
by Christopher Webb

Joseph Bell & Son

This Bristol studio was a prolific producer of good stained glass windows from its foundation in 1840. The studio was run by Joseph Bell and later by his son and grandson before being sold in 1923 to **Arnold Robinson**, whose son **Geoffrey** closed it 1996. There are many Joseph Bell stained glass windows in Somerset, sometimes signed.
SEE – *Bath Abbey*, *East Brent St Mary* and *Wrington All Saints* and many others.

Burlison & Grylls

John Burlison and Thomas Grylls were trained by Clayton and Bell and persuaded by the architects Bodley and Garner to open their stained glass studio in 1868. It was bombed out in 1945 and the business closed in 1953. Their windows are usually unsigned.
SEE – *Bath Abbey*, *East Harptree St Laurence* and *Ilminster St Mary*.

Clayton & Bell

John Richard Clayton and Alfred Bell, who was born near Wincanton, opened their studio at the suggestion of Sir George Gilbert Scott in 1855. It became one of the largest and most successful of the great Victorian stained glass firms, both artistically and commercially. They

were well known for good story telling, choice of colour, use of silver stain and canopy work. At the height of their success in the 1870s they had adopted efficient factory methods and employed some 300 people. The firm closed in 1993. Windows, many of them substantial east windows, were usually signed appropriately with a bell maker's mark.
SEE – *Bath Abbey, Buckland St Mary, Milborne Port St John, Yatton St Mary* and many others.

Sir Ninian Comper 1864-1960

'The last rose of the summer of the Gothic Revival', has been described as producing 'easily the best modern glass in England comparing very favourably with the best of old English glass'. C E Kempe and the architects Bodley and Garner were his mentors. He was in partnership with **William Bucknall** 1888-1905 and knighted in 1950. Regarding colour and light as essential for atmosphere, his windows were characterised by refined full sized figures, use of clear glass, and clarity of colour – reds, blues and greens. They are usually signed with a characteristic strawberry motif.
SEE – *Downside Abbey's Lady Chapel, East Clevedon All Saints, West Bagborough St Pancras,* and *Witham Friary.*
Two of his pupils became eminent 20th century stained glass artists – **Martin Travers**, SEE – *Bicknoller St George* and *Drayton St Catherine*; & **Christopher Webb**, SEE – *Bicknoller St George, Kingstone St John, Milverton St Michael* and *Norton St Philip.*

Hardman & Company BIRMINGHAM

John Hardman was persuaded by his friend A W N Pugin to add stained glass manufacture to his ecclesiastical metal

WEST BAGBOROUGH ST PANCRAS
St Pancras with Madonna and Child
by Sir Ninian Comper

11

works in 1845. With Wailes of Newcastle his was one of two great provincial stained glass manufacturers in the early days of the Gothic Revival and was much involved with the development of antique glass. After Pugin's death in 1852 Hardman was joined by his nephew and Pugin's son-in-law **John Hardman Powell**. The firm closed in 2008. The windows are unsigned.
SEE – *Compton Martin St Michael, East Coker St Michael, Taunton St John, Yeovil St John the Baptist* and many others.

ILMINSTER ST MARY
Archangel Gabriel and the Annunciation
by Burlison & Grylls

KILMERSDON ST PETER & ST PAUL
Jesus blessing Children by Sir Henry Holiday
for James Powell & Sons

Heaton, Butler & Bayne

Clement Heaton and James Butler formed a partnership in 1855 and were joined by Robert Bayne in 1862. They were one of the several firms which started up when demand for stained glass windows was approaching its zenith. The studio closed sometime after World War II. Their windows are usually signed.
SEE – *Batcombe St Mary, Chewton Mendip St Mary Magdalene* and *West Monkton St Augustine.*

Sir Henry Holiday 1839-1927

He designed stained glass windows for many firms but particularly for James Powell and Sons 1861-90 after Burne-Jones left to work for Morris and Company. Dissatisfied with the quality of Powell's work he started his own studio in Hampstead in 1891, which closed in 1914. He was much influenced by Burne-Jones and the Pre-Raphaelites. His windows are unsigned.
SEE – *Kilmersdon St Peter and St Paul, Minehead St Michael* and *North Petherton St Mary.*

Charles Eamer Kempe 1837-1907

A prolific producer of stained glass windows and by the end of the 19th century he had over fifty employees. Originally destined for the Church he decided because of a speech impediment to serve his Church in another way. He trained with Clayton and Bell and was much influenced by the architect Bodley, by William Morris, and by the Aesthetic Movement. Bodley's interest in the stained glass of the later Middle Ages led Kempe to make considerable use of white glass and silver staining. His windows

have been described as *'jewels of mosaic colour ... in a setting of silver and gold'*. The figures have beatific expressions and are clothed in sumptuous damask. His studio was founded in 1869 and became a key influence, particularly on Comper, F C Eden and others. He was joined latterly by his nephew **Walter Ernest Tower**. Their windows are signed with the characteristic wheat sheaf maker's mark before 1907 and a wheat sheaf and tower from 1907 until the firm closed in 1934. SEE – *Frome St John the Baptist, Horsington St John the Baptist, Wraxall All Saints* and many others.

Lavers, Barraud & Westlake
Nathaniel Lavers established a studio in 1855 and was soon joined by Francis Barraud in 1858. They originally worked with James Powell and Sons. Nathaniel Westlake, who had worked with Clayton and Bell and the architect Burges, joined them in 1868. The studio closed in 1921. Their windows are unmarked. SEE – *Bath Widcombe St Thomas à Becket, Glastonbury St John the Baptist* and *Shepton Beauchamp St Michael.*

Morris & Company
The firm was founded as Morris, Marshall and Faulkner in 1861, but became known as Morris and Company in 1875 until it closed in the 1940s. William Morris met **Edward Burne-Jones** at Oxford and they became life long friends. Both were destined for the Church but were seduced by art and architecture after a visit to France. They worked for several of the great Gothic Revival architects of the day – G F Bodley, G E Street and G G Scott – but came to reject reverence for Gothic architecture and Anglo-Catholicism. After

NORTH PETHERTON ST MARY
Nativity by C E Kempe

FROME HOLY TRINITY
Jesus as Love by Edward Burne-Jones

BUCKLAND ST MARY
Jesus confronting Soldiers by Michael O'Connor

1877 Morris refused to make glass windows for medieval buildings, for which his were arguably not entirely suited. As a consequence they lost out to the firm Burlison and Grylls, which retained an adherence to the Gothic and the traditional role of windows as an integral part of architecture rather than as decoration. Morris and Company exercised a huge influence on the development of Victorian stained glass with a concentration on simplicity, secularism and the use of particular colours – blues, rubies, yellows and especially greens. The Arts and Crafts Movement owes much to Morris and Burne-Jones. Burne-Jones, who became a baronet in 1894, was the chief artist designer. Formerly designer for Powell and Sons, he is best known for his collaboration with Morris. In his own words he *'hated the copying of ancient work as unfair to the old and stupid for the new'*. Morris is well known as founder of the Society for the Protection of Ancient Buildings. The firm flourished in the 1880s and 1890s until Morris' death in 1896 and Burne-Jones' death in 1898. Morris and Burne-Jones windows are unsigned but easily recognisable.
SEE – *Frome Holy Trinity, Huish Episcopi St Mary* and *Over Stowey St Peter & St Paul.*

Michael O'Connor 1801-1867

O'Connor learnt his trade with Thomas Willement. He practised in Dublin, in Bristol 1842-45, and in London. The studio he established closed in the 1900s. There are many O'Connor windows, which are unmarked, in Somerset.
SEE – *Buckland St Mary, East Brent St Mary, Frome St John the Baptist* and *West Quantoxhead St Etheldreda.*

James Powell & Sons

The firm, subsequently Whitefriars, was founded in 1834 when James Powell took over a firm in Whitefriars which had been making glass since the 17th century. When James died in 1840 Arthur Powell took over the firm and in 1844 opened a stained glass department, which designed and made stained glass windows. The firm was at the forefront of the development of antique glass. Although the brothers James Cotton and Nathaniel Powell did some designing the firm became well known for good design due to the association with a large number of distinguished stained glass artists, most notably Edward Burne-Jones until 1861 and then Henry Holiday until 1890. From the 1860s the firm, with a huge output, offered two qualities of window – cheaper windows made with mass produced decorative quarries and rich painted windows with antique (hand made) glass. Powell windows are usually signed with the distinctive Whitefriar maker's mark.

SEE – *Bath Abbey, Blagdon St Andrew, Hornblotton St Peter, Yatton St Mary* and many others.

William Wailes NEWCASTLE

Hardman of Birmingham and Wailes of Newcastle were the two important provincial firms in the early days of the Gothic Revival. Wailes studied in Munich with Mayer and Company and never lost the influence of German stained glass. He also worked for Pugin for a short time. The firm was set up in 1838 and from 1841 he made his own glass. In 1851 he was employing 76 people. The firm ceased trading in 1910. His windows are usually marked with an elaborate initial.

15

BATH ABBEY
L – *King Hezekiah* by Powell & Sons
R – *Jesus healing a Blind Man* by Ward & Hughes

William Wailes *continued*

SEE – *Hatch Beauchamp St John the Baptist, Norton St Philip, Taunton St Mary Magdalene* and *Wells St Thomas.*

Ward & Nixon; Ward & Hughes
The studio was started by Thomas Ward and James Nixon in 1836, but about 1850 Nixon was replaced by Henry Hughes. They produced an enormous number of stained glass windows and at the height of their fortunes employed over 100 people. However artistic standards slipped. The studio closed in the 1920s. Their windows are unmarked.
SEE – *Butleigh St Leonard* (Nixon) and *Bath Abbey* (Hughes).

Thomas Willement 1786-1871
Known by some as the *Father of Victorian Stained Glass*, he wanted to achieve the standard of stained glass which was enjoyed in the Middle Ages. He did his best to copy Medieval design with single figures beneath canopies in single lights, as at Butleigh St Leonard in 1829. His first window, an armorial window, dates from 1812. He became stained glass artist to Queen Victoria, but retired in 1865. His windows are signed with the initials TW in a shield.
SEE – *Butleigh St Leonard.*

BUTLEIGH ST LEONARD
Jesus and St John by Thomas Willement

NYNEHEAD ALL SAINTS
Georgian armorial window by John Toms

Local, national and European artists are also represented across the county, including …

LOCAL

The Horwood Brothers
MELLS AND FROME
The brothers trained in Mells at St Andrew's College founded by the Rector in 1843, and produced stained glass in the Frome area between 1857 and the 1890s.
SEE – *Frome Holy Trinity* and *Mells St Andrew*.

John Toms WELLINGTON
Toms produced stained glass in the Wellington area.
SEE – *Milverton St Michael* and *Nynehead All Saints*.

NATIONAL

Frederick Drake and Sons EXETER
The studio made several windows for Somerset churches including, probably, a delightful four-light window in *North Perrott St Martin* featuring Jesus as King lauded by musical angels.
SEE – *North Petherton St Mary*.

Alexander Gibbs 1802-1851
Father and sons designed windows for a number of Somerset churches.
SEE – *Hatch Beauchamp St John the Baptist* and *Taunton St Mary Magdalene*.

A K Nicholson 1871-1937
He designed windows for several Somerset churches.
SEE – *Batcombe St Mary, Norton sub Hamdon St Mary, and South Petherton St Peter & St Paul*. His brother the architect **Sir Charles Nicholson** designed a window for *Mells St Andrew*, or was it the artist **William Nicholson** (Foyle and Pevsner)?

Wippell and Company EXETER
This company has been producing stained glass since the early 1800s. Often designed by **George Cooper-Abbs**.
SEE – *Backwell St Andrew* and *Horton St Peter*.

EUROPEAN

Jean-Baptiste Capronnier
BRUSSELS 1814-1891
Capronnier was a medal winner at the Paris Exhibition in 1855.
SEE – *Compton Pauncefoot St Mary* and *Corton Denham St Andrew* produced in the 1860s and 1870s.

Franz Mayer and Company MUNICH
The studio influenced William Wailes and flourished from 1860 onwards.
SEE – *Huish Episcopi St Mary* and *Rockwell Green All Saints*.

17

BATCOMBE ST MARY
Archangel Michael and *Nativity* by A K Nicholson

CHAPTER FOUR

Sixty Churches

The selection of interesting churches with interesting glass is inevitably fraught with difficulty. The sixty churches listed below certainly warrant inclusion in any definitive list, but many such as Barrow Gurney St Mary & St Edward with a good collection of stained glass by C E Kempe are not included which might have been included. Dates, subject matter and names of studios are not always shown. Where approximate dates are given they usually denote the date of death of the person commemorated. Many of the windows are unsigned and therefore the maker is often unknown.

Backwell St Andrew

The church sits on an ancient site above the settlements that make up Backwell. In the chancel, the three-light east window dated c.1881 portraying Jesus in Glory, by Clayton and Bell; the three-light south window dated c.1879 portraying the Risen Jesus, probably by Joseph Bell and Son. In the north chapel, the three-light window dated 1939 portrays the Good Shepherd with armorial shields on each side. In the north aisle, the three-light east window dated c.1947 portraying St Andrew and a lad with loaves and fishes, by George Cooper-Abbs and Wippells, Exeter; a two-light window dated 1870s portraying the Adoration of the Magi, by the Camm Brothers; the three-light west window dated c.1884 depicting Abraham and the Sacrifice of Isaac, by Bell and Son. In the south aisle, the three-light west window dated c.1899 portraying Saints Paul, Luke and Barabbas, probably by Clayton and Bell.

Batcombe St Mary

A large village church with chancel, nave and two aisles St Mary's has interesting stained glass. The three-light square-headed east window with two tiers dated 1930 portraying in six panels surrounded by clear glass St Mary, Jesus enthroned, and the Archangel Michael (upper) and the Annunciation, Crucifixion, and Nativity (lower), by A K Nicholson. In the south aisle, the three-light east window portraying the Virtuous Woman (*Proverbs* XXI) and the four-light window dated 1896 portraying Saints George, Patrick, David and Andrew, both by Heaton, Butler and Bayne. In the north aisle, the three-light east window c.1910 portraying Jesus, also by Heaton, Butler and Bayne; on the north wall two three-light windows have central lights by Sally

BATH ABBEY
Scenes from the Life of Jesus
by Clayton & Bell

Pollitzer, one illustrating the Magnificat dated 2006 and the other a memorial window dated 2011. There is much decorative grisaille glass.

Bath Abbey

In spite of considerable World War II damage from bombing raids the abbey is a treasure house of 19th and 20th century stained glass, especially from the studio of Clayton and Bell. The great seven-light east window consisting of twenty-eight sections in four tiers dated 1873 is a narrative of the life of Jesus in fifty-six scenes. Although badly damaged in 1942 it has been successfully restored by the original makers Clayton and Bell. The seven-light west window consisting of twenty-one sections in three tiers dated 1865-94 depicting events from the Pentateuch (first five books of the Old Testament), also by Clayton and Bell. To view other windows perambulate clockwise starting from the north-west corner of the building. In the north aisle, the four-light west window dated 1862 portraying the four Evangelists, by W E Chance, Birmingham; five five-light windows dated 1866-72 including one depicting the Lamb of God, by Clayton and Bell, and an heraldic window dated 1951 made up of salvaged 17th century glass, by Joseph Bell of Bristol. In the north transept, two windows dated 1922 and 1924 portraying Saints Peter and Paul, and Ruth and Esther, both by James Powell and Sons. In the north choir aisle, a five-light window dated 1947-56, by James Powell and Sons; the four-light east window dated 1949 illustrating the Crowning of King Edgar by Archbishops Dunstan and Oswald, designed by Edward Woore and made by Joseph Bell. In the south choir aisle, the four-light east window dated 1952 illustrating the Consecration of the original Norman cathedral, by Joseph Bell; two five-light windows dated 1914 and 1870, one portraying Mary anointing Jesus' feet, and the other featuring Jeremiah with scenes showing the young Jesus in the Temple, by Burlison and Grylls; a five-light window dated c.1872 portraying Jesus' post Resurrection appearances, by Ward and Hughes. In the south

BATH ABBEY
L – *The Crowning of King Edgar*
by Edward Woore for Joseph Bell & Son

R – *Jesus blessing his Disciples*
by Ward & Hughes

transept, two five-light windows, one dated 1953 featuring the Archangel Michael and other Archangels from St Michael's, Folkestone, and the other dated 1914 portraying St George with Kings Arthur and Alfred, by Burlison and Grylls; the Jesse window dated 1873 showing the ancestry of Jesus, by Clayton and Bell. In the south aisle, four five-light windows dated 1868-73 including one depicting Jesus healing the sick, and another portraying Jesus with illustrations of Charity, Faith, Justice and Hope, by Clayton and Bell; a five-light window dated 1869 depicting Jesus blessing children and other scenes, by Ward and Hughes; the four-light west window portraying the builders and makers of the Temple, Moses, David, Solomon and Zerubbabel, by Joseph Bell. There is a good windows guide in the abbey shop.

Bicknoller St George

In the shadow of the Quantock Hills, St George's has an interesting selection of stained glass. In the chancel, the five-light east window with lovely colours and surrounding clear glass portraying the Risen Jesus with the Fall of Man on the left and the Crucifixion on the right, by Christopher Webb; on the north wall a three-light window depicting Paul's Conversion, also by Webb; on the south wall a three-light window dated 1930s portraying Mary and Jesus, by Martin Travers; and a four-light window portrays Saints Elizabeth, Dorcas, George and Michael. The three-light memorial west window dated 1952 illustrating the life of St Paul, by Margaret Rope.

Bishops Lydeard St Mary

Standing majestically with its impressive tower in a huge churchyard, St Mary's has a considerable collection of stained glass, especially 19th century, mostly by Lavers and Barraud c.1860s. The three-light World War I memorial east window dated 1924 portraying Mary and Jesus in the centre light, by Sir Ninian Comper. A two-light window in the south wall of the chancel portrays Jesus. In the Lady Chapel, two three-light

BICKNOLLER ST GEORGE
The Risen Jesus
by Christopher Webb

OPPOSITE – BISHOPS LYDEARD ST MARY
Madonna and Child with Bishop and St George
by Sir Ninian Comper

24

Within the window glass, the following inscriptions appear:

BEHOLD
I HAVE GIVEN
HIM FOR

A LEADER
AND
COMMANDER
TO THE PEOPLE

DAVID

JOSHUA

SOLOMON

THE GOD OF SALVATION

THE PEACEFUL ONE

TO THE GLORY OF GOD AND IN
LOVING MEMORY OF WILLIAM HENRY

LORD WINTERSTOKE OF BLAGDON
THIS WINDOW IS GIVEN BY HIS

NEPHEWS & NIECE GRAMAN & FREDK
STANCOMB AND VIOLET BURTON

BLAGDON ST ANDREW
Joshua, David and Solomon
by James Powell & Sons

windows, one dated 1938 depicting the Annunciation, by Comper. In the south aisle, three three-light windows, one portrays Jesus with Saints Peter and Paul, and the west window illustrating the Fall and Redemption, by Lavers and Barraud. In the north aisle, two windows by James Powell and Sons dated 1899 and 1903; a four-light east window portrays four saints; four three-light windows portray historical scenes and figures from the New Testament; the three-light west window with two tiers portrays Jesus with Christian symbols below. The five-light west window has decorative grisaille glass.

Blagdon St Andrew

Built by Frank Wills in the 1900s St Andrew's has a traditional matched set of stained glass windows by James Powell and Sons dated 1909-14. All are three-light windows by Powell and Sons unless otherwise stated. In the north aisle, four windows portray *Old Testament* characters – Ezra with Nehemiah and David; Isaiah with Ezekiel and Jeremiah; David with Joshua and Solomon; Moses with Aaron and Abraham. The four-light west window illustrates the early life of Jesus. The north and south aisle west windows illustrate respectively the Calling of the Fishers of Men and the Crucifixion of St Andrew. In the south aisle, three windows portray New Testament characters – John the Evangelist with John the Baptist and St Stephen; Stephen's Martyrdom; St Matthew with the Centurion and Joseph of Arimathea. The five-light east window portrays the Good Shepherd flanked by Saints Philip, Andrew, Peter and Nathaniel. In the War Memorial chapel, the south window portrays Jesus in Glory with Saints Mary and John, and the four-light east window portrays King Alfred, St George, Joan of Arc and King Edmund. There is a good windows guide in the church.

Bridgwater St Mary

A large town church with elegant spire St Mary's has a fine Jacobean Corporation pew. In the chancel, two three-light windows portray on the north side the Good Shepherd with David and John, and on the south side Jacob with Joshua and Benjamin. In the south-east St George's chapel, stained glass by Clayton and Bell; a four-light east window dated c.1880s depicting Jesus and the Acts of Mercy; and two three-light

BLAGDON ST ANDREW
Joan of Arc by James Powell & Sons

25

FOR OF SUCH IS THE KINGDOM OF HEAVEN

windows, one c.1876 illustrating the theme '*I am the Resurrection and the Life*', and the other the Crucifixion. In the south transept, the four-light east window portrays Saints Patrick, George, Andrew and David; the five-light south grisaille window has shields and medallions with arms and Christian symbols. In the south aisle, a four-light window depicts the Annunciation with the prophets Isaiah and Malachi; the three-light west window dated 1926 depicting Jesus blessing children, by Horace Wilkinson. In the north aisle, a three-light window depicts the risen Jesus with the Crucifixion below. In the north transept, the five-light north window portrays the risen Jesus with the two Marys, John the Evangelist and Joseph of Arimathea; two three-light east windows, one dated 1903 depicts Faith, Hope and Charity and the other dated c.1921 portrays the risen Jesus. The two-light west window portrays Mary and the baby Jesus.

Bruton St Mary

A Gothic gem with two towers and an unusual 18th century chancel, St Mary's has some interesting stained glass. The six-light west window dated 1888 with two tiers of figures illustrating the History of the Christian Faith, by Clayton and Bell. In the south aisle, reading from east to west, five three-light windows from different studios – Jesus' Ministry dated 1890s; faded panels surrounded by patterned quarries; the risen Jesus with hand raised in Blessing, perhaps by C C Powell, London dated 1918; Jesus as Teacher dated 1906, attributed to Clayton and Bell; the Crossing of the Red Sea dated 1890s, by the Royal Stained Glass Works. In the north aisle, a three-light window dated c.1890s portraying Jesus presiding at the Eucharist, by W F Dixon who trained with Clayton and Bell; the three-light west window dated 1890s portrays the Good Shepherd. A four-light clerestory armorial window also portrays Saints Michael and Gabriel.

Buckland St Mary

Built by Benjamin Ferrey in the 1850s and much too large for a small village, St Mary's, sometimes called the *Cathedral of the Blackdowns*, is lavishly furnished with fine stained glass windows. In the chancel, the five-light east window and two three-light windows dated 1857 illustrating scenes from the life of Jesus, by

BRUTON ST MARY
Jesus ministering to those in need.
Unattributed

28

TO THE GLORY OF GOD AN OFFERIN

ROM MY HIGHLY ESTEEMED AN

RTLY BELOVED BROTHER

W L TVRNER BD LATE FELLOW O

Michael O'Connor. In the north aisle, a two-light window dated 1914 portraying the Saints Michael and George, by Kempe and Tower; a three-light window dated c.1859 and a two-light window illustrating the Acts of Mercy, by Clayton and Bell; and two other two-light windows, one commemorating the builder of the church portrays David and Solomon. In the vestry, a four-light window dated 1857 and fading badly, by James Powell and Sons. In the south aisle, two two-light windows, one depicting the Annunciation by Kempe and Tower and the other by Powell and Sons. The six-light west window dated 1859 illustrating the Last Judgement, by Clayton and Bell. In the tower, a four-light window c.1860s illustrating the Crossing of the Red Sea, by Clayton and Bell, as are two windows opposite on the north wall, one a two-light window with a carpentry scene from Nazareth, and the other a single light window illustrating the Baptism of Jesus.

Butleigh St Leonard

Lying in the shadow of Butleigh Court, St Leonard's has some significant stained glass windows. In the chancel, the three-light east window dated 1829 portraying Jesus with his Mother Mary and St John, by Willement, an important early example of the revival of stained glass windows as in the Middle Ages with figures beneath canopies in the main lights and representative symbols, for example the Holy Dove, in the tracery lights; two two-light windows one portraying Jesus the Shepherd instructing his disciples and the other the Risen Jesus with Mary, the latter dated 1880s and showing Arts and Crafts influence. In the south transept, a three-light window dated 1853 portraying the Risen Jesus, by Ward and Nixon, and a single light dated 1846 portrays Mary and Jesus as a boy. In the north transept, a three-light

BUCKLAND ST MARY
The Last Judgement by Clayton & Bell

BENEDICTUS FRUCTUS VENTRIS TUI

30

window dated 1880s illustrates Faith, Charity and Hope, and a single light portrays St Leonard. In the nave, on the south side a three-light window dated 1851 portraying St Peter with John the Baptist, by A W N Pugin, and a two-light window dated 1870s illustrating the Annunciation with delightful musical angels, by Hardman and Company. In the north aisle, a two-light window dated 1920 illustrating Jesus calming the Storm, by Horace Wilkinson.

Charlton Mackrell St Mary

The church guide book quotes an unnecessarily disparaging description of the windows as *'the least said the better'*. There are several decorative grisaille windows some with small medallions or roundels, and in the vestry six attractive small diaper lancet windows. Three chancel windows were destroyed by a bomb in World War II, one of them replaced by a memorial medallion dated 2005 in the central light of a three-light window with a local scene by Andrew Johnson of Stonecroft Stained Glass. On the north wall a three-light window dated 1849 illustrating scenes in the early life of Jesus, by Joseph Bell of Bristol. In the north transept, a five-light memorial window dated 1860 portrays Mary and Jesus with other scenes from the lives of Jesus and a selection of saints. Unfortunately the three-light window in the south transept with three panels surrounded by clear glass is hidden from view by the organ.

Chewton Mendip St Mary Magdalene

A dark church inside but its tower is one of the tallest and most splendid in Somerset. The three-light east window dated c. 1865 (fading badly) illustrating the Crucifixion, by Robert Bayne of Heaton, Butler and Bayne. Most of the other stained glass windows dating from c.1880 and later are also by Heaton, Butler and Bayne. In the south chapel, a three-light east window dated 1880 illustrates Faith, Love and Hope. On the north wall two two-light windows illustrate the themes *'Feed my Lambs'* and *'Jesus praying in the Garden of Gethsemane'*; and a three-light window portrays the Good Shepherd with Saints Peter and John, all by Cox and Buckley dated late 19th century. In the south aisle, two

BUTLEIGH ST LEONARD
Annunciation by Hardman & Company

three-light windows dated 1882 illustrating scenes from the life of Jesus; a two-light window portrays Jesus as the Light of the World, by Heaton, Butler and Bayne; and a three-light west window portrays Jesus at Bethany. The four-light west window illustrates two post-Resurrection scenes, the Empty Tomb and the Appearance on the road to Emmaus.

Compton Martin St Michael

Perhaps the best Norman church in Somerset, St Michael's has some good Hardman and Company stained glass windows, including two in the porch dated 1943 portraying Saints Christopher and Barbara. In the chancel, the three-light east window dated 1902 illustrating the Transfiguration of Jesus, by Murray of London; three single light decorative windows, one dated 1871 with roundels illustrating the Beatitudes, by J H Powell, and two with emblems of the Evangelists, by William Wailes. Above the chancel arch a three-light window portraying St Michael. In the north aisle, three three-light windows dated 1943-50, all by Hardman, depicting the Archangels; Mary and Jesus with Joseph and Joseph of Arimathea; Saints Andrew, Wulfric and George. In the clerestory, four single light windows dated 1943-50, all by Hardman, portray, reading for west to east, St Jerome, Ethelred, Edward the Confessor, and Thomas à Becket. There are other decorative windows.

Compton Pauncefoot St Mary

Attractively situated close to the substantial Georgian rectory, the church with an elegant spire has, for a small village, an impressive collection of stained glass. Five three-light windows dated 1864-77 by Jean-Baptiste Capronnier of Brussels in his striking pictorial style with bold design and vivid colours – blues, reds and greens – illustrate the Crucifixion (east window), the Nativity and John the Baptist (south aisle), and Jesus' concern for children and his Death, Resurrection and Ascension (north aisle). There are eight Capronnier windows in nearby Corton Denham St Andrew. A three-light west window dated 1896 portraying three Archangels, by C E Kempe. In the chancel, two two-light Blackford family memorial windows dated 1948, by

COMPTON PAUNCEFOOT ST MARY
John the Baptist and Jesus by J-B Capronnier

Hugh Easton. In the north aisle a three-light window traditional in design portrays saints. Two decorative windows with geometric designs, by the Whitechapel Glass Works.

Crewkerne St Bartholomew

This cruciform market town church with central tower and majestic turreted west front is one of Somerset's best. In the chancel, the five-light east window dated 1897 portraying Jesus in Glory with Saints Mary, John, Michael and Gabriel, by Clayton and Bell; on the north wall, a four-light window portraying Jesus teaching, by Percy Bacon; on the south wall, three four-light windows (from the east) one dated c.1928 portraying the Risen Jesus, by Percy Bacon; one dated 1958 portraying St Cecilia with a portable organ and the theme 'Sing unto the Lord', by Christopher Webb; one patterned grisaille window with two central panels featuring the Angel and the Three Women at the Empty Tomb, by Ward and Hughes. In the north-east chancel aisle, a colourful five-light east window dated 1880 portraying Jesus with children and illustrating the Acts of Mercy, by Alexander Gibbs; two four-light windows one dated 1928 portraying Saints Mary, Elizabeth, Mary Cleopas and Salome, and the other dated 1925 illustrating the Good Samaritan parable, both by Percy Bacon. In the north transept, three panels of a five-light east window dated 1961 depicting the Lamb of God with the Tree and River of Life, by Marion Grant. In the nave, on the north wall a superb six-light window dated 1894 illustrating the Nativity with the Shepherds and the Magi in attendance, by Hardman and Company; and on the south wall a six-light window dated c.1884 showing Jesus teaching and healing, by Hardman and Company. In the south transept, a four-light east window dated 1908 portraying David and Jonathan, by Hardman and Company. The seven-light west window with two tiers dated 1930 portraying Jesus in Glory and a Tree of Learning from the Old Testament to the New Testament with twenty-five saints and angels, by A K Nicholson. There are several clear glass windows which let in plenty of light.

Dunster St George

Once divided between the Benedictine monks and the parishioners of Dunster, St George's has one of the best chancel screens in the south-west of England. East of the screen, the three-lancet east window, reconstructed by G E Street, illustrating the Crucifixion and other scenes, by Clayton and Bell. In the south east chapel, the three-light east window with two tiers illustrates the Burial and Resurrection of Jesus, and two armorial grisaille windows. In the south aisle, a three-light window portrays Jesus the Teacher, by Clayton and Bell. West of the screen, in the nave, a four-light west window with two tiers dated 1886 illustrating scenes from the New Testament, by Clayton and Bell. In the south aisle, four three-light windows (reading from east to west) illustrate Jesus blessing children, by Heaton, Butler and Bayne; Jesus teaching, attributed to Clayton and Bell; the Baptism of Jesus dated c.1875, by Clayton and Bell; and the Adoration of the Magi dated 1876, by Clayton and Bell. There are several patterned grisaille and clear glass windows.

East Brent St Mary

With its elegant spire St Mary's has a number of stained glass windows by Joseph Bell, including two of the several three-light windows in the north wall of the north aisle, panels with grisaille surrounds portraying Jesus' disciples, John the Baptist and St Paul. In the chancel, the three-light east window portraying Jesus, by Michael O'Connor; three two-light windows on the south wall illustrating scenes from the life of Jesus, one designed by Mary Miles and made by Joseph Bell; and a two-light window dated 1930s on the north wall. In the north aisle, the three-light 15th century east window restored in 1852 by Joseph Bell illustrates the Crucifixion, and the three-light west window with two tiers portraying six Prophets also by Joseph Bell which was formerly the east window. On the south wall, a three-light window portrays the Virgin Mary with Saints Mark and Luke. There are patterned grisaille windows in the south transept.

East Clevedon All Saints

Built by C E Giles in 1860, All Saints is particularly well endowed with stained glass, especially by Sir Ninian Comper. Perambulating clockwise from the west end, on the north side all the windows are by Comper unless otherwise stated – a two-light Benedictus window dated 1923 portraying John the Baptist; in the Baptistry, two three-light windows dated 1918 celebrate

N GRATITVDE FOR 25   Y^{RS} OF HAPPY & BLESSED   MINISTRY F·F·I· 1924

Baptism and the Eucharist; a three-light window dated 1880 illustrating the Sermon on the Mount, attributed to Clayton and Bell; a three-light window dated c.1867 portraying Jesus calming the Storm, probably by Lavers, Barraud, and Westlake; a two-light window dated 1918 portraying Saints Stephen and Alban. In the north transept and chancel aisle, a three-light Jesse window dated 1924, a wheel window dated 1913 by Hunt of Clifton. In the chancel, a three-light east window date 1901 portraying Jesus in Majesty, by C E Kempe; two two-light windows dated 1916 portraying the Fathers of the Church, Saints Jerome, Gregory, Ambrose and Augustine, and a single light dated 1917 portraying St George, all by Comper. In the south transept and Lady Chapel, a two-light Annunciation window dated 1903, by Kempe; three single light windows – an Angel, by Jean-Baptiste Capronnier of Brussels dated 1872, and Saints Edward the Confessor and Swithin dated 1922. In the south aisle, a two-light window dated 1927 portraying Saints Agnes and Catherine, by F C Eden; a three-light window dated 1860s portraying Jesus on the way to Calvary, by Clayton and Bell; a three-light window dated 1860s illustrating the Wise and Foolish Virgins, by William Wailes; a three-light window dated 1874 with panels illustrating scenes from the life of Jesus, by Capronnier; a three-light window dated 1860s portraying the Good Shepherd, by Clayton and Bell; and a two-light Magnificat west window dated 1923 portraying the Virgin Mary and Elizabeth, by Comper. The west rose window dated 1920, by Comper. The eight clerestory windows by an unknown artist illustrate the Passion and Crucifixion. Heraldic windows in the porches. There is an excellent church guide.

East Coker St Michael

Overlooking open countryside by Coker Court, St Michael's is associated with the poet T S Eliot whose ashes are buried in the churchyard and with the navigator William Dampier. The four-light east window dated c.1866 illustrating aspects of the life of Jesus, and the three-light Bullock (a family of sailmakers) memorial west window dated c.1885, both attributed to Hardman and Company. In the chancel, two three-light windows portraying archangels, and in the north transept a three-light Bullock memorial window dated 1920s, all by James Powell and

FROME HOLY TRINITY
The Good Shepherd, the Ascension, and Evangelists
by the Horwood Brothers

34

Sons. In the Eliot corner in the north aisle, a three-light window dated 1936 illustrating Faith, Love and Hope and commemorating the Eliot family's emigration to Massachusetts c.1660, by Leonard Walker. In the south transept, a two-light memorial window with panels remembering six local worshippers, by the Jasper and Molly Kettlewell Studio, set up at Coker Court for a short time in 1984.

Frome Holy Trinity

This aisleless church built in the 1830s has a remarkable set of twelve single light stained glass windows designed by Sir Edward Burne-Jones and made by Morris and Company 1880-1921. The five windows on the liturgical north wall portray the Good Shepherd and the four Gospel writers. The three west windows portray Saints Catherine, John the Baptist and Paul. The four windows on the liturgical south wall portray Jesus as Love, St Peter, Jesus blessing Children, and Jesus stilling the Storm. The three-light liturgical east window dated 1875 depicting the Good Shepherd and the Ascension in the centre with the Evangelists and St Paul on either side, by the Horwood Brothers of Mells and Frome. There is a good windows guide in the church.

Frome St John the Baptist

On the hillside in the centre of the town St John's was much altered in the 19th century, particularly by C E Giles 1862-5. In the chancel, the five-light east window dated c.1865 illustrating the Crucifixion, by Clayton and Bell; and a north window by Michael O'Connor. In the south chapel, the three-light east window dated 1846 portraying Bishop Ken and Jesus the Shepherd, by Michael O'Connor; a two-light window dated 1840s, by William Wailes. In the north chapel, two two-light windows illustrating the Annunciation, Adoration and other scenes, and one five-light window dated 1923-4, the latter portraying the Madonna and Child and other scenes, all by C E Kempe and Company; the two-light west window dated c.1964 illustrating the Fall and the Nativity, unattributed. In the south aisle, a lancet window dated 1985 commemorating the foundation of the church, by Mark Angus; one three-light window portraying John the Baptist and King Herod, and five

FROME ST JOHN THE BAPTIST
The Visitation of Mary to Elizabeth
by C E Kempe

WHATSOEVER HE SAITH UNTO   YOU DO IT S JOHN II V 5   I AM THE GOOD SHEPHERD   RISE TAKE UP THY BED

two-light windows dated 1929 depicting John the Baptist preaching, the Baptism of Jesus, and John the Baptist's captivity, death and burial, all by Kempe and Company; the four-light west window with Biblical scenes, unattributed. In the north aisle, three two-light windows dated 1924-30, depicting Gabriel and Zacharias, the Visitation of Mary to Elizabeth, and the naming of John the Baptist, by Kempe and Company; a window dated c.1865, by Arthur O'Connor. The four-light abstract west window by Mark Angus.

Glastonbury St John the Baptist

Described by Leland in 1534 as *'a fair lightsome church'*, St John's with its splendid tower has some interesting stained glass. The seven-light east window with two tiers dated 1879 illustrating the Crucifixion and Resurrection with portraits of the four Evangelists includes some 15th century glass, by Nathaniel Westlake. In the north chancel aisle, a five-light window dated 1885 portraying John the Baptist, by Westlake. In the south chancel aisle, two five-light windows dated c.1880 depicting scenes in the life of Jesus, by Westlake. In the north transept, a four-light window dated 1936 portraying in particular Joseph of Arimathea and his alleged visit to Glastonbury, by A J Davies, Bromsgrove. In the south transept, a five-light window with two tiers dated 1924 depicting Glastonbury saints and scenes including St Dunstan who was born nearby, in the centre upper light St Michael with the Scales of Judgement and in the centre lower light St George slaying the dragon, possibly by Daniells and Fricker, partly cartooned by George Daniels who was for many years cartoonist for Clayton and Bell before working on his own, freelance; a four-light window with two tiers dated 1867 portraying Noah, Moses, Elijah and John the Baptist, by Clayton and Bell; and a two-light memorial window dated 1857 with roundels illustrating the symbols of the Evangelists.

Hatch Beauchamp St John the Baptist

Situated away from the village in the grounds of Hatch Court, St John's has a good selection of 19th century stained glass. The

L – GLASTONBURY ST JOHN THE BAPTIST
The Good Shepherd and other scenes from the Life of Jesus
by Nathaniel Westlake

R – HATCH BEAUCHAMP ST JOHN THE BAPTIST
An Act of Mercy by Alexander Gibbs

three-light east window depicting the Crucifixion and the Nativity and Baptism of Jesus, by Lavers and Barraud. In the chancel, the two-light north window dated c.1872 portrays Jesus as the Lamb of God; the three-light south window dated 1899 portraying the Good Shepherd with Saints George and Alban, by Burlison and Grylls. In the south aisle, the three-light west window dated c.1860 illustrating the Acts of Mercy, signed by Alexander Gibbs. The four-light west window dated c.1860 depicting scenes from the life of Jesus, by Gibbs. In the north aisle, the three-light west window dated 1845, by William Wailes, and two three-light windows dated c.1870s all portraying Jesus, perhaps by Joseph Bell.

Hinton St George

St George's with its unique Paulet chapel, home to some outstanding memorials, has two good windows by Clayton and Bell – the five-light east window dated 1883 illustrating the Ascension and Resurrection appearances of Jesus and in the south aisle the five-light east window dated 1916 illustrating the Passion of Jesus. In the chancel, two grisaille windows dated 1922, by J C Bewsey. In the south aisle, a four-light window dated c.1961 portraying St Francis, by Goddard and Gibbs; a two-light window depicting Mary at the empty Tomb, by Clayton and Bell; and a three-light window dated 1915 portraying Saints Dunstan, George and Alphege, by Clayton and Bell. In the Paulet chapel, a four-light window dated 1858 illustrating scenes from the life of King David, by Charles Gibbs.

Hornblotton St Peter

Built in 1872-74 by Sir Thomas Jackson for the hymn writing rector Godfrey Thring, this significant Victorian church lies just off the Fosse Way far removed from the village but close to the substantial former rectory. The stained glass windows were designed by Jackson and made by James Powell and Sons. In the chancel, the striking five-light east window portrays the Crucified Jesus between accompanying angels, some with green and some with blue wings; three lancet windows, all dated c.1891, portray Sarah, Saint Elisabeth and Lois. Under the tower, the two-light west window illustrates the Baptism of Jesus; two lancet windows portray the Ethiopian Eunuch and the Centurion

Cornelius; two small lancets in the west wall portray the heads of Simeon and Anna. In the nave four two-light clear glass windows with patterned leading let in ample light.

Horsington St John the Baptist

Rebuilt 1886-7 St John's has a fine series of stained glass windows by C E Kempe, especially the four-light east window, dating from the rebuild, portraying Jesus and the Forerunner John the Baptist. In the chancel, three single light windows portray John the Evangelist, James, and Peter (both the latter badly faded). On the north wall of the nave, three two-light windows depict (from the east) scenes from the Garden of Eden to the Descent from the Cross; scenes from the life of St Paul; Saints Francis and Martin. In the south aisle, four two-light windows, three by Kempe, illustrating (from the east) the Annunciation dated 1886; the Baptism of Jesus dated 1923; Jesus carrying the Cross dated 1908; the fourth illustrates the Adoration by the Shepherds in the style of Kempe possibly by Herbert Bryans. There are some unexciting patterned grisaille windows.

Huish Episcopi St Mary

With one of the finest towers in Somerset, the subject of a postage stamp in 1972, St Mary's is now the parish church of Langport as well as Huish Episcopi. The three-light east window dated 1876 depicts the Crucifixion. In the chancel, one window dated c.1913 depicts the Annunciation, and a two-light window dated 1930 shows Jesus in the arms of Simeon (illustrating the Nunc Dimittis), by Morris and Company. In the south chapel, the four-light east window dated 1904 illustrating the Nativity, by Sir Edward Burne-Jones and Morris and Company. In the north transept, the three-light north window in striking colours with a background of royal blue dated 1871 illustrating Jesus as My Beloved Son, by Michael O'Connor; the three-light descriptive east window dated 1883 depicting Mary and the other women at the empty Tomb, by Mayer and Company, Munich. There is a good collection of windows dated c.1900 by Mayer and Company in Rockwell Green All Saints. On the north wall of the nave, a three-light window depicts the Ascension with Jesus blessing Saints Mary, Peter and others.

HORSINGTON ST JOHN THE BAPTIST
Tha Adoration by the Shepherds
Kempe style, possibly by Herbert Bryans

Ilminster St Mary

An impressive Perpendicular centre of town church St Mary's is built on a cruciform plan complete with crossing tower. The five-light east window dated 1888 portraying Mary and baby Jesus with the Crucifixion beneath, Gabriel and St John on the left and Athanasius and Isaiah on the right, by Burlison and Grylls. In the south transept, the three-light west window dated 2007 commemorating the Old Ilminsterians, by John Reyntiens. In the north transept, the three-light east window with two tiers dated 1964 portraying St Catherine, by Christopher Webb. In the nave, three three-light windows on the south side, one dated 1902 illustrating the Nativity, another showing the boy Jesus in the Temple disputing with the Learned Doctors, and the third dated c.1905 showing Jesus in His Father's carpentry shop; two three-light windows on the north side, one dated c.1893 illustrating the Ascension, and the second illustrating the Crucifixion, signed by Heaton, Butler and Bayne. The five-light west window dated c.1908 portrays Aldhelm, Catherine, Alfred the Great, Cecilia and Bishop Ken.

Kilmersdon St Peter & St Paul

Situated by the main road in the centre of the village the church has a number of fine windows designed by Sir Henry Holiday and made by James Powell and Sons. They include the three-light east window dated 1880 portraying Mary and Jesus, reminiscent of the work of Sir Edward Burne-Jones; in the north aisle, two three-light windows, one dated 1886 illustrates Jesus' Baptism and the other dated 1890 illustrates Jesus' devotion to children; in the south wall of the nave a lancet window, and a two-light window illustrates the Annunciation. In the north aisle, the four-light east window dated 1914 portraying musicians, by Louis Davis; a three-light west window dated 1860s illustrates scenes from the life of Jesus.

Langport All Saints

Situated on high ground overlooking the Levels towards Muchelney Abbey, All Saints is in the care of the Churches

L – ILMINSTER ST MARY
St Catherine by Christopher Webb

R – LANGPORT ALL SAINTS
Old Testament Worthies by Hugh Kennedy

ABRAHAM   IOB   DAVID   MOSES   SOLOMON

IN HONOR OF   GOD & LOVING   MEMORY OF   WALTER SON   OF THOMAS
WATSON & EDITH   BAGEHOT OF   HERDS HILL   HE DIED   MARCH XXIV
MDCCCLXXVII   AGED LI   ERECTED BY   HIS WIFE ELIZA   BAGEHOT

MELLS ST ANDREW
Madonna and Child and St Francis with Birds and Fish
by Sir Charles Nicholson

Conservation Trust. The five-light east window dated 1867 with ten portraits containing much Medieval glass, restored by Clayton and Bell. In the south-east chapel, the four-light east window dated c.1865 illustrates Justice, Charity, Prudence and Virtue; two four-light windows, one dated c.1861 portrays the four Evangelists, and the other illustrating the Acts of Mercy, by Alexander Gibbs. In the south aisle, the three-light east window dated 1868 showing Jesus blessing children, by Michael O'Connor; a three-light window dated c.1887 in memory of a wife who died in India. In the north aisle, a three-light window dated 1904 illustrating Faith, Hope and Charity, by James Powell and Sons; a single light memorial west window dated c.1935, by A K Nicholson, includes a view of Wells Cathedral. The richly coloured five-light west window in memory of Walter Bagehot, the historian and essayist, who is buried in the churchyard, portrays Abraham, Job, David, Moses and Solomon, by Hugh Kennedy. There are several plain glass lead patterned windows.

Mells St Andrew

In one of the finest settings in Somerset and with its Horner connection, St Andrew's has splendid furnishings, including some interesting stained glass. In the chancel, the three-light east window dated 1882 portraying Jesus enthroned, by Hardman and Company; two three-light windows, one dated 1882 portraying Melchisidec with Abel and Abraham, by the Horwood Brothers, and the other portrays Saints Peter, John and James. In the north chapel, the splendid three-light east window dated 1930 portraying the Blessed Virgin Mary and St Francis with birds and fish, by Sir Charles Nicholson. In the chapels and aisles, eight three-light windows, badly fading, portraying Old Testament and New Testament characters, by the Horwood Brothers. The five-light west window dated 1851 portraying the Evangelists, by Hudson. The clerestory windows have patterned grisaille glass.

Milborne Port St John

With stonework dating to Saxon and Norman times St John's church has a fine series of Clayton and Bell windows. The four-light east window dated 1910 portraying Mary and Jesus with the Archangel Michael, John the Evangelist and St George, by

Bainbridge Reynolds. In the south transept, two single light windows portray the Agony in the Garden, and in bright colours Jesus as the Shepherd. In the nave, four three-light windows dated 1869 illustrating scenes from the life of Jesus, the most easterly the Raising of Lazarus and the most westerly the Draught of Fishes miracle, all by Clayton and Bell except possibly the latter. The five-light west window in two tiers dated 1969 illustrating scenes from the life of Jesus with the bottom tiers concentrating on the Nativity, by Clayton and Bell.

Milverton St Michael

Standing proudly at the top of the village the red sandstone church has an important collection of Medieval bench ends. In the chancel, the four-light east window celebrating Victory and dated 1951 portraying Jesus carrying the Cross with Mary Magdalene and Saints Michael and George, by Christopher Webb; on the south wall a three-light window dated 1850 portrays St George with Saints Peter and Paul; on the north wall a two-light window portrays John the Baptist and St Stephen. In the south aisle, a four-light window dated c.1877 illustrates in detail four parables of Jesus – the Good Samaritan, the Labourers in the Vineyard, the Ten Talents, and the Wise Steward, by Hardman and Company; above the door a three-light window portrays the risen Jesus. In the north aisle, a three-light window dated 1907 depicts St Michael and accompanying angels. There are several windows by John Toms of Wellington dated 1849-50 – patterned quarries with coloured borders, one a four-light window with roundels showing the emblems of the four Evangelists.

Minehead St Andrew

A busy town centre church built by G E Street in 1880, St Andrew's has a particularly fine five-light east window dated 1887, by C E Kempe. It depicts the Crucifixion with Saints George and Mary on the left and John and Andrew on the right. Below are Old Testament Prophets and above in the tracery lights symbols of the Passion. The colours, reds and blues, and the use of silver stain with a light architectural background are typically Kempe. In the north aisle, a two-light window dated 1933 illustrates the

43

MILBORNE PORT ST JOHN
Madonna and Child with Archangel Michael and St John
by Bainbridge Reynolds

Visit of the Magi. In the south-east annexe, a two-light window dated 1938 portraying Saints Nicholas and Ursula, signed by Christopher Webb, St Albans. There are a number of clear glass windows with appropriately styled amber borders.

Minehead St Michael

The church stands majestically on the side of a steep hill overlooking the town and the bay with fine views towards Dunster. In the chancel, the four-light colourful (reds, blues and greens) east window dated c.1901 illustrating twelve scenes from the life of Jesus from the Nativity to the Ascension, by Sir Henry Holiday; two three-light windows dated c.1905 and c.1917 portray respectively Jesus with children, and Mary with baby Jesus and Saints Michael and George; in the Rood staircase, a single memorial light. In the nave, a four-light window dated c.1913 portrays Saints Joseph of Arimathea, Christopher, Catherine of Siena and Francis of Assisi. In the north aisle, a four-light east window with two tiers dated 1902 illustrating the Annunciation and the Adoration by the Shepherds, by C E Kempe; a three-light window dated c.1914 portrays Saints Martin, Michael and George; a four-light window dated c.1927 with central panels portrays Simeon and Anna.

North Petherton St Mary

A fine centre of village church with a superb tower, St Mary's has a particularly good C E Kempe window. In the chancel, the five-light east window dated c.1885 depicting the Ascension of Jesus, and two three-light windows with two tiers dated 1880s portraying twelve figures including St Paul and some of the Apostles, probably by Frederick Drake and Sons of Exeter; a third three-light memorial window to two brothers killed in World War I dated 1918 portraying Jesus the Good Shepherd, by Sir Henry Holiday. In the north chapel, the three-light east window with two tiers dated 1896 illustrating the Nativity, known locally as the *Christmas Window*, by Kempe. The four-light west window with two tiers dated 1911-13 with scenes from the life of Jesus, probably by Clayton and Bell.

Norton St Philip

Winner of the *Country Life Magazine* Village Church for Village Life

44

MINEHEAD ST MICHAEL
The Adoration of the Magi by Sir Henry Holiday

Award in 2008, the church has some interesting windows. In the chancel, the five-light east window dated 1929 illustrating the Nativity, by Christopher Webb; the two chancel windows dated 1850, by William Wailes. In the south aisle and chapel, three three-light windows, one dated c.1870 portraying Jesus instructing his disciples, by Joseph Bell; and one dated c.1890 portraying Jesus with the words '*I am the Resurrection and the Life*', by Clayton and Bell; the west window illustrates the Baptism of Jesus. In the north aisle and chapel, the four-light east window portrays fifteen angels including three in the tracery lights against a background of patterned foliage; two three-light windows, one dated c.1890 illustrates the Acts of Mercy, the other dated c.1873 portrays Eunice, Anna and Dorcas; the three-light west window dated c.1882 portrays the Risen Jesus in Glory. The three-light grisaille west window incorporates roundels with symbols of the Evangelists and the Paschal Lamb and Pelican in her Piety.

Norton sub Hamdon St Mary

Nestling below Ham Hill, St Mary's is a fine compact Perpendicular church with an unusually tall tower. In the chancel, the four-light east window with two tiers dated 1861 illustrating the life of Jesus, by William Wailes; the three-light south window dated 1875 portraying Jesus blessing children by Heaton, Butler, and Bayne; the three-light north window dated 1922 portraying Jesus as the Sower of Good Seed, by A K Nicholson. In the south chapel, the three-light east window dated 1904 commemorating the Golden Wedding of Charles and Susan Trask and portraying Our Lady with the idealised family Vita, Caritas and Labor, designed by Henry Wilson and made by Shrigley and Hunt, Lancaster. On the north wall, the four-light World War I memorial window portrays Saints George and Michael with regimental badges. The four-light west window with two tiers has a floral pattern and clear glass, by Henry Wilson.

Nynehead All Saints

In the shadow of Nynehead Court, All Saints has rich furnishings including windows (a good collection by John Toms of Wellington) thanks to the munificence of the Revd John Sanford. In the chancel, the three-light east window dated 1869 with the

NORTON SUB HAMDON ST MARY
Our Lady and the personification of Work
by Henry Wilson for Shrigley & Hunt

OLD CLEEVE ST ANDREW
Jesus with St Andrew by Sir Ninian Comper

figure of Jesus in the central light with patterned lights on either side, by Heaton, Butler and Bayne; on the south wall a two-light window, dated early 19th century portraying Faith in red and Hope in white, and on the north wall a lancet window portraying a bishop with a gold mitre, both designed by Sir Joshua Reynolds in the 18th century portrait style. In the south aisle, the four-light east window dated c.1860s portraying fourteen saints, by Frederick Drake of Exeter; two three-light windows with Saints James and Mary Magdalene in the central lights with patterned grisaille lights on either side; a striking three-light domestic armorial Georgian window with 16th century glass having a shield in the central light with a gold lion and a red dragon as supporters, put in by Toms in 1851; the two-light west window illustrating the Baptism of Jesus by Toms. The three-light west window dated 1887 illustrating the Annunciation, by James Powell and Sons. In the north aisle, two three-light patterned windows dated c.1900 with portrait medallions of Wycliffe, St Francis, Dante, Saints Paul, Clement of Alexandria and Augustine of Hippo, by Powell and Sons. In the north chapel and organ chamber, two two-light armorial windows, and two wheel windows dated 1869, by Heaton, Butler and Bayne. There is a good church guide.

Old Cleeve St Andrew

Overlooking the Bristol Channel towards Minehead, St Andrew's has an impressive variety of stained glass windows. In the chancel, the three-light east window dated 1953, by Sir Ninian Comper; a two-light window dated 1898 portraying Saints Peter and Andrew, by C E Kempe. In the south aisle, the two-light east window dated c.1897 portraying Saints Mary and John the Evangelist, by Morris and Company; the three-light west window with two tiers dated c.1905 showing scenes from the life of Jesus with Biblical texts, by Sir Henry Holiday. In the nave, a two-light Millenium window with a local flavour, by Minehead artist Frankie Pollak. The four-light west window illustrating scenes from the life of Jesus, by Lavers and Barraud.

Over Stowey St Peter & St Paul

In a secluded village at the foot of the Quantock Hills, the church has some good Morris and Company stained glass windows. In

and gorth befurr you info galilre

the chancel, the three-light east window dated 1857 depicting the Crucifixion, by Hardman and Company; four single light windows portray Saints Peter and Paul and two incidents in the life of Jesus. In the north aisle, the two-light east window dated 1870 showing Mary at Jesus' tomb, and the four-light west window dated 1874 portraying angel musicians, both designed by Sir Edward Burne-Jones and made by Morris and Company; two three-light windows, one illustrating Faith, Hope and Charity, and in the south aisle two three-light memorial windows, all attributed to Morris and Company. In the tower, a three-light window illustrates scenes in the life of Jesus.

Portishead St Peter

A much restored and reordered Perpendicular church with a tall tower and some fine glass. In the chancel, a four-light east window portraying Jesus Crucified and in Glory, and two three-light windows, one on the north side showing the Raising of Lazarus with Faith, Hope and Charity below, and the other on the south side showing Jesus healing with Truth, Chastity and Fortitude below, all dated 1860s, by Clayton and Bell; a three-light window dated c.1857 portraying the Risen Jesus in bright colours, by Lavers and Barraud. In the nave south side, a three-light window dated 1885 portraying Jesus as the Good Shepherd, and a two-light window dated 1928 portraying Saints Cecilia and Luke, by Joseph Bell and Son, as is the four-light east window dated 1879 in the north-east vestry; a fine three-light window in dark blues, reds, greens and purple dated 1904 illustrating the Benedictus canticle, Zacharias' Song of Thanksgiving at the birth of his son John the Baptist, by Arts and Crafts artist Mary Lowndes. In the north aisle, two four-light windows dated 1920s, one portrays St Mary and Jesus as the Light of the World with two apostles, and the other Saints Peter, Luke, John and Nicholas.

Selworthy All Saints

Described by Arthur Mee as 'a church perfect in beauty', a sentiment repeated by F C Eeles,1876-1954, the Founder and first Secretary of the Council for the Care of Churches, who is commemorated by a window in the church, All Saints stands out in its white coat of limewash with a commanding view towards Exmoor. The

OVER STOWEY ST PETER & ST PAUL
Mary Magdalene at Jesus' Tomb
by Sir Edward Burne-Jones

three-light east window dated c.1863 illustrating six scenes from the life of Jesus, by Clayton and Bell. In the south aisle, patterned grisaille windows with coloured borders, one featuring the Seven Marks of the Holy Spirit. In the north aisle, four three-light windows (from the east); one dated c.1924 portraying Saints Anne, Barnabas and Dunstan, by Sir Ninian Comper; one dated 1956 commemorating F C Eeles, by Christopher Webb; one dated c.1896 portrays Jesus; one dated 1958 portraying Saints Alban and Francis, by Christopher Webb.

Shepton Beauchamp St Michael

This splendid church with a fine tower lies in the centre of the village. In the chancel, the three-light east window dated c1870 depicting the Crucifixion, by Clayton and Bell; and three two-light windows dated c1860-70 illustrating Mary's visit to the Tomb of Jesus; the Annunciation and Nativity; and the Ascension and Coming of the Holy Spirit, all by Clayton and Bell. In the south aisle, the three-light east window dated 1880s portraying Jesus with arms raised in blessing, by Philip, brother of Nathaniel Westlake; and two three-light windows and a two-light west window all dated 1888-97 illustrating the miracle of the Turning of the Water into Wine at the Marriage Feast of Cana; the Visit of the Wise Men to baby Jesus with a scene showing the execution of a Christian martyr in Central Africa; and the Baptism of Jesus, all designed by J F Bentley and made by Lavers and Westlake. In the north aisle, the three-light east window dated 1923 portraying the Madonna and Child accompanied by Isaiah and Athanasius, by Christopher Webb; the two-light west window dated 1865 portraying Saints Stephen and Alban, by Hudson of London. The four-light west window with two tiers has figures in the four central panels, one showing St Michael slaying the Dragon. This window came from the chancel following the G E Street reordering in the 19th century.

South Petherton St Peter & St Paul

A large church in the centre of the village with a distinctive octagonal central tower and some fine stained glass windows in the south aisle by A K Nicholson. In the chancel, the four-light east window with two tiers dated 1882 has eight figures including Moses, Saints John the Baptist, Peter and Paul,

SHEPTON BEAUCHAMP ST MICHAEL
Madonna and Child with Christian Martyr in Central Africa
by J F Bentley for Lavers & Westlake

48

probably by Clayton and Bell; on the south side, a two-light window dated c1880 portraying the Risen Jesus, by Hardman and Company, and three-light window dated 1887 illustrating three miracles of Jesus, including the Raising of Lazarus, probably by Clayton and Bell; on the north side, a two-light window illustrating the Nativity and the Crucifixion, by Hardman and Company, and three-light window dated 1912 depicting the Virgin Mary, by A K Nicholson In the south aisle, the three-light east window dated 1920s illustrates the Adoration of the Shepherds; two three-light windows dated 1925-26 portraying King Ina with his wife Ethelburga and Bishop Birinus; and King Alfred with Aldhelm, Bishop of Sherborne, and Dunstan, Archbishop of Canterbury and their associated buildings, all by A K Nicholson. The five-light west window with two tiers dated c.1875 illustrating the lives of Jesus and the church's patron saints Peter and Paul, by Clayton and Bell. In the north aisle the three-light west window has a Millenium central light featuring the Holy Spirit, by Joanna Dover.

Taunton St John

One of Somerset's Victorian gems, St John's built by Sir George Gilbert Scott at a cost of £12,000 was dedicated in 1863. The three-lancet east window illustrating key incidents in the life of Jesus, and the three-light west window illustrating the Transfiguration, both designed by John Hardman Powell and made by Hardman and Company for £130 and £125 respectively. In the north Lady Chapel, the east wheel Gospel window depicting the emblems of the four Evangelists by Clayton and Bell, and the three-light north window c.1884 showing Jesus blessing children, possibly by Burlison and Grylls. In the north-west Baptistry, a wheel window, and two single lights dated 1914 featuring sixteen well-known saints, including Peter and Andrew on the west wall and Augustine and Ambrose on the north wall, the latter two windows designed by Dudley Forsyth and fitted by Hartnell of Taunton.

Taunton St Mary Magdalene

St Mary's with its double aisles and phenomenally tall tower rebuilt by Benjamin Ferrey and Sir George Gilbert Scott in 1858-62 has much fine stained glass. In the chancel, the seven-

SOUTH PETHERTON ST PETER & ST PAUL
Bishop Aldhelm and Sherborne Abbey
by A K Nicholson

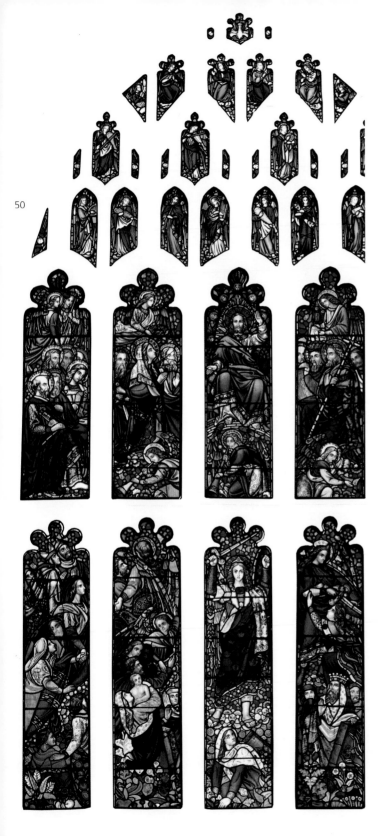

50

light east window illustrating the Passion and Crucifixion and the three-light south window portraying Saints Peter, Mary Magdalene and Joseph of Arimathea, both dated 1887 for Queen Victoria's Golden Jubilee, by Clayton and Bell; the heraldic clerestory windows, probably by Wailes. In the south chapel, the four-light east and two three-light south windows, dated 1890s, illustrating respectively six scenes from the life of Jesus and six saints, by Clayton and Bell; a three-light window in painterly style, the earliest in the church dated c.1845, with a roundel flanked by Saints Simon and Andrew, by local artist William Ray. In the south aisle, the five-light east window with two tiers dated 1912 portraying ten local and national heroes, by A L Moore; three three-light windows in the south wall dated 1900s illustrating respectively Saints Martin, George and Alban; the Risen Jesus; and Chivalry, Fortitude and Faith, by Clayton and Bell; two four-light windows in the south wall illustrating respectively the four Evangelists, and Saints John of Chrysostom, Mark, George and Denis, by Wailes; the west World War I memorial window dated 1920. The bold and colourful five-light west window with two tiers dated 1862 illustrating the Last Judgement, by Alexander Gibbs. In the north aisle, two three-light windows, one dated 1920 illustrating the Nunc Dimittis with Simeon holding the baby Jesus; the other portraying Jesus as King.   There is a good stained glass guide by Dr Jim Cheshire.

Trull All Saints

The church is richly furnished with a superb pulpit, fine bench ends and interesting glass. The much restored three-light 15th century east window illustrating the Crucifixion with equally precious Medieval stained glass next to it in the so-called Dragon window. Four three-light windows dated c.1880s, two in each of the aisles, illustrate the Te Deum canticle, for example in the south aisle the apostles Matthew, Peter and Thomas; and the archangels Gabriel, Michael and Raphael. In the south aisle, the three-light east window dated 1865 illustrating the events of the Passion 'I am the Resurrection and the Life', by the Horwood Brothers; a three-light window on the south wall dated 1876 illustrating six scenes from the life of Jesus, by Lavers, Barraud and Westlake; the three-light west window dated 1964 portraying Saints Luke, Paul and Mark, by J S Bucknall, the last commission

TAUNTON ST MARY MAGDALENE
The Last Judgement by Alexander Gibbs

from the Comper studio. In the north aisle, the three-light west window dated 1913 portraying Saints James, Elizabeth and Peter, by Kempe and Tower; the three-light north window dated 1899 portraying Saints Martin, Machar and Nicholas, by Kempe, and donated by the Scot Alexander Ewing, who wrote the tune for 'Jerusalem the Golden'.

Wells St Thomas

This handsome Victorian church built by S S Teulon in 1857 for £6,000 has some fine grisaille and clear glass windows. The north aisle vine patterned green glass windows by Thomas Wilmshurst have been restored using glass from the south aisle, which has clear glass with attractive lead patterns. In the south aisle, the four-light decorative grisaille west window dated 1866, attributed to Richard Clayton of Clayton and Bell. In the north aisle, a single light west window portrays Jesus with Mary Magdalene. The glory of the church lies in the chancel with five two-light windows by William Wailes. They imitate the typological lay-out of the Middle Ages with Old Testament scenes on the left and complementary New Testament scenes on the right – (from north to south) Noah and the Ark with the Baptism of Jesus; Joseph sold to the merchants with Jesus' Betrayal; Moses and the serpent in the wilderness with the Crucifixion; Abraham and Isaac with the Resurrection; Elijah taken to Heaven in a chariot with the Ascension. On the south wall of the chancel a three-light window portrays St Thomas.

West Bagborough St Pancras

Situated by the manor house, St Pancras has fine stained glass windows and furnishings by Sir Ninian Comper. Most of the stained glass windows dated 1920s and 1930s are by Comper. In the chancel, the three-light east window dated 1922 portrays the Virgin Mary with Saints Pancras and Dunstan; and a single light depicts two child angels and a naked child Jesus. In the vestry, two two-light windows portray the Annunciation and the Archangels Michael and Raphael. On the north wall two two-light windows and on the south wall two two-light windows portray various saints and worthies; a three-light window

WELLS ST THOMAS
Elijah taken to Heaven with the Ascension of Jesus
by William Wailes

portrays Saints Joseph of Arimathea, George and Alban. Two other windows portraying Jesus, one a two-light in the chancel and the other a three-light on the north wall of the nave, unattributed.

West Monkton St Augustine

With a tall and for Somerset an unusually plain tower, St Augustine's is tucked away from the centre of the village. Most of the stained glass windows are by Heaton, Butler and Bayne. In the chancel, the three-light east window dated 1884 illustrating the Crucifixion with the Nativity and the Appearance of the Risen Jesus on the road to Emmaus, by Clayton and Bell; the three-light south window dated c.1900 portrays Jesus as the Shepherd and Light of the World. In the south-east chapel, the three-light window dated 1898 showing the Risen Jesus appearing to Peter, John and the women, by Heaton, Butler and Bayne. In the south aisle, three two-light windows two dated 1880s illustrating Mary at the Empty Tomb and the parable of the King's Wedding Feast, by Heaton, Butler and Bayne, and the third portraying the Presentation of baby Jesus to Simeon and Anna, by Heaton, Butler and Bayne; the two-light west window dated c.1885 illustrating the parable of the Publican and the Pharisee, by Heaton, Butler and Bayne. In the north aisle, three three-light windows, two illustrating the Ascension, and Reflections on Psalm 23 in memory of a boy who died aged sixteen, by Heaton, Butler and Bayne; and the third shows Jesus in Glory with Saints Peter and John; the two-light west window shows the young Jesus in the Temple with the Scribes, by Heaton, Butler and Bayne.

West Quantoxhead St Etheldreda

Also known as St Audries, this Victorian church built in 1856 lies on the edge of woodland between the Quantock Hills and the Sea. In the chancel, the three-light east window a colourful representation of the Crucifixion, by Michael O'Connor; on the south wall, two single lights illustrating four scenes in the life of Jesus, by O'Connor; in the north chancel aisle, a two-light east window illustrating the Annunciation, and two single lights portraying Saints Mary and Etheldreda, by O'Connor. In the south aisle, a three-light east window dated 1882 portraying

Jesus with Saints Peter and John, by C E Kempe; a two-light window dated c.1938 portrays Saints Elizabeth of Hungary and Theresa of Avila. In the north aisle, a two-light west window depicting the Baptism of Jesus, by Hardman and Company. The four-light west window dated c.1903 portrays the four Archangels with four New Testament scenes beneath. There are a number of attractive windows with patterned quarries and coloured borders.

53

Weston-super-Mare All Saints

This unfinished Bodley church opened in 1902 has a fine south aisle extension by F C Eden. In the chancel, the five-light east window dated 1917 illustrating the Crucifixion with saints and kings, by C E Kempe; a two-light window portraying Saints Thomas Aquinas and Anselm, by Eden. In the south aisle chapel, the four-light east window dated c.1925 portraying saints, by Eden; the three-light south window dated 2002 illustrating the Crucifixion, by Alan Thomas and the Gilroy Studio, Bristol using Eden's glass dated 1933 from the redundant St Saviour's church. In the south aisle, a three-light window dated 1926 portraying three women, designed by Leonard Pownall and made by Liddall Armitage, and a single light west window dated 1924 portraying King Oswald of Northumbria. In the north aisle, a single light memorial west window dated 1953, by Harry Stammers.

Wincanton St Peter & St Paul

This substantial town church with nave and three aisles was rebuilt by J D Sedding in 1887-9. The five-light east window dated 1891 illustrating the Te Deum canticle, by Clayton and Bell. In the inner south aisle, a four-light window dated c.1898 with scenes of the Risen Jesus. In the outer south aisle, two three-light windows, one dated c.1896 depicts the Building of the House of God, and the other dated 1898 illustrates the Benedicite canticle, a theme of Praise with musical instruments; also a three-light World War I memorial window portraying the Risen Jesus with the promise of Resurrection and the Crown of Life, by James Powell and Sons. The two-light west window

The goodly fellowship

The glorious company

The noble army

of the Prophets

of the Apostles

of Martyrs

praise thee

praise thee

praise thee

54

portrays Jesus blessing children. In the north aisle, two three-light windows, one portraying Mary and baby Jesus with Isaiah and St Luke, and the other a war memorial window dated 1921 portraying St George, by Morris and Company.

Winscombe St James

A particularly fine church in an equally fine setting overlooking the vale to the north, St James has an extensive collection of Medieval stained glass. The restored Medieval windows include, in the chancel the three-light Carsleigh window, in the north aisle the four-light east window and the most easterly three-light window, and in the south aisle the most easterly three-light window. In the chancel, the eye-catching east window of three lancets dated 1863 portraying Solomon, David and others in a stylized Jesse tree with attractive background, by William Burges; a single light painterly south window illustrates a mother nursing a child. In the north aisle, a three-light window with patterned quarries; a three-light window dated c.1900 portraying three saints; and a three-light west window dated c.1888 depicting Charity, Hope and Faith. In the south aisle, four three-light windows (reading from the east) the second dated 1896 portraying Saints James the Less, John and Peter, by Joseph Bell and Son; a window with geometric patterns and a family crest; two windows dated 1882 and 1879 illustrating Jesus' teaching including the Acts of Mercy and the parable of the Good Samaritan, by Lavers, Barraud and Westlake. The four-light patterned grisaille west window with faded panels illustrates the life of Jesus, especially his concern for children.

Witham Friary St Mary, St John the Baptist & All Saints

An aisleless relic from monastic days this church has in the south wall four delightful windows dated 1923 illustrating the life of St Hugh, Prior of Witham 1179-86 and later Bishop Lincoln, by Sir Ninian Comper. The three-light east window dated 1909 portraying Jesus in Majesty with St Thomas a Becket and St Hugh, by James Powell and Sons.

L – WINCANTON ST PETER & ST PAUL
An illustration of the Te Deum Canticle by Clayton & Bell

R – WITHAM FRIARY
St Hugh, Bishop of Lincoln by Sir Ninian Comper

56

Wiveliscombe St Andrew

This spacious fully-pewed red sandstone church was built by the west country architect Richard Carver in 1829 though the sanctuary was remodelled in 1872. In the sanctuary, the rose window, ridiculed by Pevsner as *'uncongenial and unattractive'*, illustrating St George (according to the church guide, or is it St Michael?) and the Dragon, and two two-light windows dated 1915 portraying the four national patronal saints – George, Andrew, Patrick and David – by Alice Erskine. In the north aisle, the three-light east window (from the former church) dated c.1893 with scenes from the life of Jesus; a four-light window dated c.1891 portraying eight Biblical heroines; a five-light window fading badly dated c.1874 illustrating the Crucifixion and other scenes; a four-light window dated c.1887 portraying the four Evangelists, all by Clayton and Bell; the three-light west World War I memorial window dated 1916 illustrating the Crucifixion with saints, by C E Kempe. In the south aisle, the three-light east window dated 1922 illustrating a Jesse Tree 'in honour of the Holy Incarnation', by Kempe; a four-light window dated c.1860s (from the original chancel) illustrating Jesus carrying the Cross, the Crucifixion, the Women at the Tomb of Jesus, and the Risen Jesus; and in the clerestory, a four-light window dated c.1891 portraying Jesus as the Shepherd.

Wraxall All Saints

With its magnificent tower, All Saints is blessed with furnishings, including stained glass windows, of outstanding quality due to the munificence of the Gibbs family of nearby Tyntesfield. All the windows, except for two in the chancel by C E Tute, are by C E Kempe, dating from 1896 to 1899 when his studio was at the height of its competence and popularity. They form a coherent scheme starting with three three-light windows in the north aisle depicting the Annunciation, Nativity, and Visit of the Magi. Two three-light windows in the north transept illustrate Jesus' Presentation in the Temple and Visit to the Doctors. In the

L – WIVELISCOMBE ST ANDREW
St Andrew by Alice Erskine

R – WRAXALL ALL SAINTS
Jesus as King in Majesty by C E Kempe

chancel, the five-light east window portrays Jesus in Majesty with saints and angels, and two two-light windows by Tute illustrate the Entombment and the Resurrection. In the south 'Charlton' chapel, three three-light windows illustrate the Passion and Crucifixion. On the south wall of the nave, a three-light window with clear glass surrounds depicts the Baptism of Jesus. The three-light west window portrays St Michael slaying the dragon.

Wrington All Saints

An impressive Perpendicular church situated in the centre of the village All Saints is well lit by some fine stained glass windows. In the chancel, the five-light east window dated 1860 portraying the Good Shepherd and scenes from the life of Jesus, by Joseph Bell of Bristol; two three-light windows, one on the north wall dated c.1884 a memorial to Hannah More portraying Faith, Charity and Hope, and the other on the south wall dated c.1876 illustrating the Last Supper, both by Clayton and Bell. In the south aisle, the four-light east window dated 1879 portraying Jesus the Teacher, by Joseph Bell; four four-light windows (reading from the east) the Risen Jesus with Peter and others dated 1891, by Mayer and Company, Munich; eight episodes in the life of Jesus dated 1872, by Clayton and Bell; Jesus the Healer dated 1909, by Powell and Sons; the Raising of Lazarus and symbols of the Evangelists dated 1874, by Clayton and Bell. In the north aisle, two four-light windows, one dated 1879 depicting Jesus teaching and illustrating the Beatitudes, by Clayton and Bell, and the other dated 1859 illustrating the Annunciation and portraying Zacharias, by Joseph Bell. The six-light west window with two tiers dated 1859 portraying eighteen saints and showing Renaissance influence, by Joseph Bell. There are grisaille clerestory windows by Joseph Bell.

Yatton St Mary

With its truncated spire and splendid Perpendicular south porch, St Mary's has some fine glass by Clayton and Bell. In the chancel, the five-light east window dated c.1887 portraying the Risen Jesus with Saints Mary, Mary Magdalene, John and Joseph of Arimathea; and three two-light windows on the south side, one

YATTON ST MARY
The Carpenter's Shop. Jesus' home in Nazareth
by Clayton & Bell

dated 1877, illustrating scenes from the life of Jesus, by Clayton and Bell; on the north wall a two-light window dated c.1865 illustrating the Adoration of the Magi, by Henry Hughes. In the north chapel, the four-light east window dated 1928-9 illustrating the Annunciation and the Crucifixion with St Mary and St John, and on the north wall two three-light windows dated 1951 portraying the Risen Jesus, by James Powell and Sons. In the north aisle, two good four-light narrative windows, one dated c.1900 illustrating Jesus preaching from a boat on the Sea of Galilee and the other dated 1926 illustrating Jesus' home, the Carpenter's Shop in Nazareth, both by Clayton and Bell. There are several windows with clear quarries.

Yeovil St John the Baptist

A major centre of town church of harmonious design sometimes known as the *Lantern of the West*, St John's has a number of stained glass windows by Hardman and Company. The four-light east window dated 1863 displaying scenes from the Passion (events leading up to the Crucifixion), and the four-light west window dated 1852 in memory of Prince Albert displaying scenes from the life of John the Baptist, both by Hardman and Company. In the north aisle, a four-light window dated 1919 illustrating St Michael and Victory over Evil, by Sir Henry Holiday. In the north transept and north choir aisle, three five-light windows one dated 1879 costing £250 illustrating the Ascended Jesus in Glory; the east window dated 1862 illustrating the Resurrection appearances of Jesus, both by Hardman and Company, the third dated 1874 illustrating the Last Judgement, unattributed. In the south aisle, three five-light windows, the east window dated 1859 costing £155 7s 6d illustrating Jesus' Miracles of Healing, by Lavers and Barraud; the other two dated 1859 illustrating scenes from the life of Jesus, by Hardman and Company. In the south transept, a five-light window dated 1862 costing £210 depicting the Last Supper showing Judas with thirty pieces of silver and a black halo, by Hardman and Company. Above the south porch, a five-light Gloria window, unattributed. There are several patterned grisaille windows some with medallions showing Christian symbols.

YEOVIL ST JOHN
Judas Iscariot with the black halo at the Last Supper
by Hardman & Company

CHAPTER FIVE

Recent Commissions

The commissioning of stained glass windows continues. Here follows a selection of some twenty of the artists and their stained glass windows which adorn Somerset churches. Some likely windows have not been included, for example at Wick St Lawrence a three-light east window dated 1989 portraying Jesus blessing children by Michael Lassen. All the windows mentioned have been installed since World War II, many of them in the last decade or so. Designed to let in as much light as possible, all are dedicated to the Glory of God though the glory of man is usually evident. Some are representative and illustrate traditional subjects – Biblical themes or lives of saints; others reflect the secular age in which we live – celebrating the countryside, or attempting to create an atmosphere conducive to worship or an understanding of Faith. Most are adornments rather than parts of the Gothic architecture in which they often sit unhappily, placed as they are alongside more traditional stained glass.

FROME ST JOHN
Commemoration window by Mark Angus

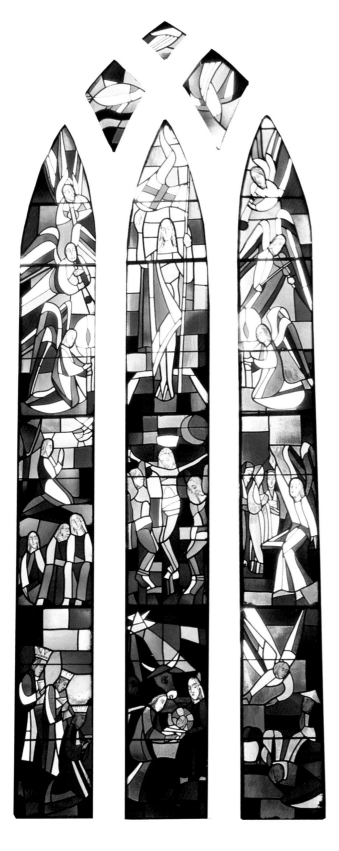

Mark Angus
A number of abstract windows in Somerset churches including *Bath St Stephen* a three-light window representing St Stephen dated 1979; in *Cheddon Fitzpaine St Mary* a three-light window dated 1988 representing the Four Seasons; in *Claverton St Mary* a memorial window dated 1983; in *Frome St John* a four-light west window dated 1989 and a single light window commemorating the church's 900th anniversary; in *Westfield St Peter* four sanctuary windows dated 1982.

61

Gunter Anton Stuttgart, d.1989
In *East Chinnock St Mary* nine windows in a distinctive naïf narrative style dated 1962-88 illustrating the life of Jesus – given in gratitude for being so well treated locally as a prisoner of war in World War II.

Stewart Bowman
In *Pendomer St Roch* a three-light window dated 2003 portraying St Roch, described by the assessor in a disputed Faculty application as *'a pleasant and suitable east window for a charming little church'*; in *West Coker St Martin* a two-light window dated 2001 portraying Saints Christina and Martin.

Fran Davis, Unicorn Glass
In *Priddy St Lawrence* a two-light memorial window dated 1990 portraying Jesus surrounded by animals and birds; in *Ashwick St James* a window yet to be installed.

EAST CHINNOCK ST MARY
Scenes from the Life of Jesus by Gunter Anton

62

MILTON CLEVEDON ST JAMES
The Tree of Wisdom by Tom Denny

Tom Denny
In *Milton Clevedon St James* a three-light abstract window dated 1996 illustrating the Tree of Wisdom from Proverbs Chapter III. He is well known nationally amongst others for his windows in *Gloucester Cathedral*.

Hugh Easton 1906-65
In *Compton Pauncefoot St Mary* two two-light memorial windows, one commemorating Lord Blackford and the other his two children killed in World War II; in *North Cheriton St John the Baptist* a three-light window dated 1961 portraying an uncommonly youthful St John the Baptist.
Well known for the east window of the RAF Chapel in *Westminster Abbey*, he is commemorated by a window in *Bradford-on-Tone St Giles*.

Roger Fyfield
In *Congresbury St Andrew* a three-light south aisle west window dated 1971 showing Jesus blessing children in pleasing red, green and yellow colours.

John and Laura Gilroy
In *Biddisham St John the Baptist* a two-light Millenium west window; in *South Barrow St Peter* a three-light Millenium east window. Both windows feature barley and grapes. In *Publow All Saints* a three-light Millenium north aisle west window with a local flavour.

Jane Gray
In *Pitminster St Mary & St Andrew* a striking four-light east window dated 1989 illustrating the Calling of St Andrew; in *Bradford-on-Tone St Giles* a window yet to be installed.

truly whoever does not accept the kingdom of
so like a child shall not enter it

FOLLOW
ME

PITMINSTER ST ANDREW
The Calling of Andrew by Jane Gray

CONGRESBURY ST ANDREW
Jesus blessing children by Roger Fyfield

Goddard and Gibbs

In *Hinton St George* a delightful four-light window portraying St Francis; in *Westfield St Peter* two superb tall windows from the demolished Cachmaille-Day church of 1953 illustrating the Draught of Fishes – '*I will make you fishers of men.*'

David Gubbin

In *Horton St Peter* five single-light windows dated 1990s portraying Saints Cecilia, Francis, George, Jerome and Peter.

Henry Haig d. 2008

In *Staplegrove St John* an abstract Millenium window featuring rising flames; in *Nailsea Holy Trinity* a window yet to be installed. He is well known nationally for many church commissions.

John Hayward 1929-2007

In *Blackford St Michael* a three-light east window dated 2002 portraying Jesus as the Good Shepherd, a window of which this well-known artist was particularly proud; in *Sutton Montis Holy Trinity* a three-light Millenium west window with a local flavour. He is well known nationally and locally, not least for his west window in *Sherborne Abbey*.

Julie Hibbert

In *Kingston St Mary*, where she lives, a three-light abstract window in the chancel dated 1994 depicting the mantle of Mary with the motif of Healing.

Edward Nuttgens 1892-1982

In *Pitney St John the Baptist* a three-light window dated c.1977 portraying Stephen Hardinge (born in Somerset and later Abbot of Citeaux, Cistercian abbey in France) and St John the Baptist on either

WESTFIELD ST PETER
Fishers of Men by Goddard & Gibbs

BLACKFORD ST MICHAEL
The Good Shepherd by John Hayward

side of the Holy Spirit. Born in Aachen he married an English girl and settled in Buckinghamshire where he established a nationally and internationally esteemed studio at High Wycombe close to the studio of Eric Gill. He was much influenced by Christopher Whall and the Arts and Crafts Movement.

Sally Pollitzer
In *Batcombe St Mary* the centre lights of two three-light windows, one illustrating the Magnificat dated 2004, and the other dated 2009 commemorating the death of a local girl at a sadly young age.

John Potter
In *Litton St Mary* a three-light Millenium west window depicting a Tree of Life with themes of Hope and ongoing Creation.

Patrick Reyntiens OBE
In *Stoke St Mary* three fine representational two-light windows depicting St Anne teaching St Mary, Pentecost, and the Annunciation; in *Taunton St George* (Roman Catholic), with his son **John**, a magnificent five-light west window portraying Christos Pantocrator. This world renowned artist, who recently completed eight huge windows in the restored medieval church of *Cochem St Martin* in Germany, lives near Ilminster and is well-known for his work with John Piper at *Coventry Cathedral*. In *Ilminster St Mary* a commemorative window by John, who designed the circular window in the Catholic church of South Petherton and the heraldic window in *Westminster Hall* celebrating the Diamond Jubilee of Queen Elizabeth II.

BATCOMBE ST MARY
The Magnificat by Sally Pollitzer

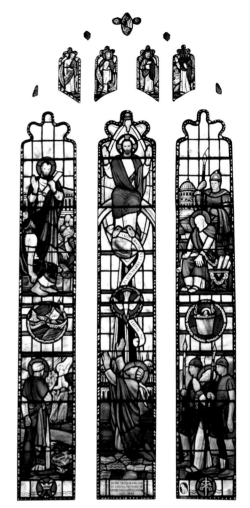

BICKNOLLER ST GEORGE
The Life of St Paul by Margaret Rope

Margaret Rope 1891-1988
In *Bicknoller St George* a three-light memorial west window dated 1952 illustrating the life of St Paul. Known as Tor as opposed to Marga, one of two Arts and Crafts cousins, both called Margaret and both stained glass artists.

Brian Thomas
In *Drayton St Catherine*, in the north aisle, a three-light memorial window dated 1976 portraying St Catherine.

CHAPTER SIX

Some Indulgences

Finally there are a score of interesting or favourite windows which have not been mentioned or which seem to fit none of the sections of this celebration of stained glass in Somerset parish churches. Some of these are mentioned in the previous chapter.

Ansford St Andrew
A three-light Woodforde commemorative east window dated c.1856 illustrating the Crucifixion and the Nativity and Baptism of Jesus. The Revd James Woodforde, author of *The Diary of a Country Parson*, was born in 1740 in Ansford, where his father was rector. Also a three-light west window dated c.1926 portraying Mary and baby Jesus.

Bath, Lansdown St Stephen
On the south wall of the nave, a tall two-light window with eight cameos, including Albert Schweitzer, Elizabeth Fry, Saints Francis, Boniface and Alphege, set in an entwining vine, by Arnold Robinson, a pupil of Christopher Whall and owner of Joseph Bell & Son from 1923. Also much

BATH LANSDOWN ST STEPHEN
Six 'Saints' by Arnold Robinson

66

other interesting 19th and 20th century glass, including a three-light window by Mark Angus.

Bath Widcombe St Thomas à Becket

A three-light west window, known locally as the *'Harvest Window'*, dated 1861, with three colourful panels of flowers on a light background of blackberries and thorns, by Lavers and Barraud with the design attributed to J Milner Allen. See also the five-light east window and five two-light windows all colourful with trees and plants but with no human figures – a most interesting botanical set.

Bathampton St Nicholas

In the Australian chapel, so called because Captain Arthur Phillip, the founding Governor of New South Wales is buried in the church, two two-light clear glass windows with the coats of arms of the Commonwealth of Australia and the six States.

Bradford-on-Tone St Giles

In the north aisle, a two-light window dated 1913 portraying St Giles, patron of the church and of cripples and the poor, and St Boniface, missionary to Germany in the 7th century, who was born at or near Crediton, by Alice Erskine in the Arts and Crafts style. Also a two-light window dated 1967 commemorating Hugh Easton 1906-65, stained glass artist, and James Easton 1796-1871, Taunton engineer, by Gerald Coles, Luton; and three-light west window dated 1859 illustrating the Presentation of Jesus in the Temple, by John Toms.

Burnham on Sea St Andrew

In the chancel, a two-light window dated

67

1918 portraying Jesus with the Disciples, and in the south St Nicholas chapel a two-light window dated c.1918 portraying Jesus with Mary Magdalene, both by A J Davies, Bromsgrove.

Camerton St Peter

In the north chapel, a three-light window c.1865 depicting Jesus extending a blessing to a group of people including, unusually, a shackled negro, attributed to Michael O'Connor. Also several windows by Joseph Bell, including the three-light east window of the organ chamber in which you find two mice at the feet of St Mary in the central light.

Carhampton St John the Baptist

A four-light east window dated 1907 illustrating the Last Supper in rich colours with John the Baptist, St Paul, and the four Evangelists portrayed in the tracery lights.

Claverton St Mary

A three-light east window in Arts and Crafts style dated 1904 the theme *Come to Me*, and in the north chapel a two-light window portraying Jesus and Mary, by Paul Woodroffe. Also in the chancel a two-light window dated c.1921 portraying St Francis, by Alice Erskine; in the nave a two-light window dated 1907 the theme *Cantate Domino*, depicting musicians, by Herbert Alexander; under the tower a single light memorial window dated 1983 the theme '*I will lift up mine eyes unto the hills*', by Mark Angus.

Congresbury St Andrew

In the south aisle three unusual three-light World War II memorial windows dated 1949 dedicated respectively to

the Navy, the RAF and the Army and illustrating aspects of their respective roles, in the style of A L Wilkinson. Also a three-light west window in the south aisle dated 1971 portraying Jesus, by Roger Fyfield.

Curry Rivel St Andrew

An unusual and spectacular five-light west window dated 1865 illustrating the Nativity with the adoring Magi and Shepherds in Renaissance rather than Gothic style perhaps using German glass, by Francis Penrose, Surveyor of St Paul's Cathedral. Also in the chancel, eight panels of etched glass, a memorial dated 1987, by Laurence Whistler, in a four-light window.

Drayton St Catherine

A three-light east window in the north aisle dated 1936 portraying Mary and baby Jesus with interesting local scenes by Martin Travers. Also in the north aisle, a three-light memorial window dated 1976 portraying St Catherine by Brian Thomas; and a three-light west window dated 1912 portraying six figures including Alfred the Great, Queen Victoria, Milton and General Gordon.

East Harptree St Laurence

A three-light World War I memorial window on the south wall dated 1919 portraying Saint George with Laurence and Agnes, by Karl Parsons. Also in the north aisle four three-light windows dated c.1917-18, attributed to Burlison and Grylls.

Kingstone St John

A three-light east window portraying Jesus with Saints Anne and Florence,

DRAYTON ST CATHERINE
Madonna and Child by Martin Travers

69

KINGSTONE ST JOHN
Elizabeth and John the Baptist
by Christopher Webb

and in the chancel a two-light south window portraying Elisabeth with her son John the Baptist and St James the epistle writer and brother of Jesus, both by Christopher Webb and dated 1924. Both windows in this humble church fulfil admirably the functions of stained glass windows – they let in light, they adorn, they illuminate with their symbols and Biblical texts, and they commemorate worthy individuals.

Lympsham St Christopher

A three-light east window, dated 1863 and signed by Michael O'Connor, the theme being *Suffer Little Children* with portraits of the rector J H Stephenson's family – he was also lord of the manor, therefore a typical *squarson* of the time.

Maperton St Peter & St Paul

A three-light east window with three charming panels, the central one portraying the Virgin Mary with baby Jesus, on a light background of patterned quarries with colourful borders, dated 1869, designed by Sir Henry Holiday and made by Powell and Sons – the whole adorning the Sanctuary with a jewel like quality. A typical and appropriate east window, especially for a small church, by one of the great studios.

North Cadbury St Michael

A fine five-light east window dated 1876 portraying Jesus in Glory with Saints Gabriel and Michael and nine scenes involving angels in the main lights and the twelve Apostles in the twelve tracery lights, by Clayton and Bell, one of the most successful 19th century stained glass studios. A very typical and suitable east window,

MAPERTON ST PETER & ST PAUL
Mary Magdalene annointing Jesus' feet
by Sir Henry Holiday for James Powell & Sons

NORTH CADBURY ST MICHAEL
Archangel Gabriel and Angels
by Clayton & Bell

especially for a large church and one
dedicated to St Michael the Archangel.

Stowell St Mary Magdalene
A five-light east window with obvious
Arts and Crafts influence dated c.1912
depicting the Crucifixion with symbols
of the Christian Faith and the Evangelists
by Alice Erskine, whose work can also
be seen in Claverton St Mary, Halse St
James in a four-light window portraying
Jesus in Glory surrounded by named
saints, and Wiveliscombe St Andrew.

Taunton St Andrew
In the centre light of a three-light
window in the north aisle a commemoration of the Great Western Railway
dated 2002, by local artist Clare Maryan
Green. Also other stained glass windows
many by Lavers and Westlake post 1893
including a five-light Te Deum east
window; a three-light east window in
the Lady Chapel illustrating the Acts
of Mercy; and a three-light south-west
window illustrating the Transfiguration,
by Hardman and Company.

Taunton St James
A fine three-light east window with
two tiers dated 1860 illustrating the
Nativity and Crucifixion, by Clayton
and Bell. Also a west window dated
1875, by Heaton, Butler and Bayne;
and four windows in the south aisle
dated 1886-91 illustrating episodes
in the life of Jesus, by Swain
Bourne, Birmingham.

STOWELL ST MARY MAGDALENE
St Mary at the Crucifixion
by Alice Erskine

OVERLEAF – BATH ABBEY
Scenes from the Life of Jesus
by Clayton & Bell

Index

75

SOMERSET

OUR MAP shows the location of all the
churches which are featured in this book
and serves well to illustrate the wealth of
beautiful glass found throughout
the county . . .

76

Portishead
Wraxall
East Clevedon
Backwell
Yatton
Congresbury
Wrington
Weston-super-Mare
Blagdon
East Harptree
Winscombe
Compton Martin
Litton
Lympsham
Biddisham
Chewton Mendip
East Brent
Priddy
Burnham-on Sea
Wells
Claverton
Bath
Bathampton
Camerton
Norton St Philip
Kilmersdon
Mells
Frome
Witham Friary
Selworthy
Minehead
Dunster
Carhampton
Old Cleeve
West Quantoxhead
Bicknoller
Over Stowey
Glastonbury
Milton Clevedon
Batcombe
Bridgwater
Hornblotton
West Bagborough
Kingston St Mary
North Petherton
Butleigh
Ansford
Bruton
Bishops Lydeard
Charlton Mackrell
North Cadbury
Wiveliscombe
West Monkton
Langport
Pitney
Wincanton
Milverton
Bradford-on-Tone
Taunton
Huish Episcopi
Compton Pauncefoot
Maperton
Nynehead
Trull
Curry Rivel
Drayton
Blackford
Stoke St Mary
Hatch Beauchamp
Horsington
Pitminster
Stowell
South Petherton
Shepton Beauchamp
Norton-sub-Hamdon
Yeovil
Milborne Port
Buckland St Mary
Horton
Ilminster
Kingstone
Hinton St George
East Chinnock
East Coker
Pendomer
Crewkerne

READERS' NOTES . . .

. . . .
. . . .
. . . .
. . . .
. . . .
. . . .
. . . .
. . . .